Stepping Up To
DR DOS 6.0

by Volker Sasse

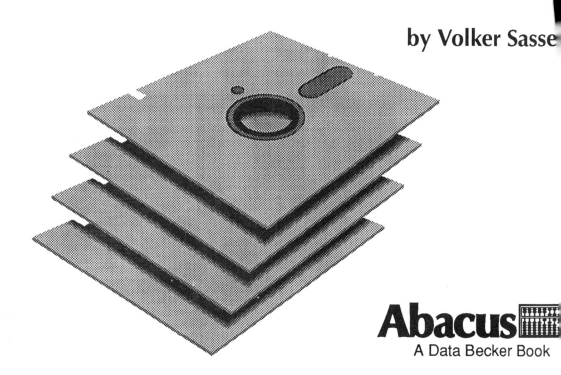

Abacus
A Data Becker Book

Library of Congress Cataloging-in-Publication Data

```
Sasse, Volker,  1958-
        Stepping up to DR DOS 6.0 / Volker Sasse.
        p.  cm.
        Includes index.
        ISBN 1-55755-129-4 : $ 14.95
        1. Operating systems (Electronic computers) 2. DR DOS.  I Title.
QA76.76.063s356  1991
005.4'46--dc20                                          91-35180
                                                          CIP
```

Printed in U.S.A.
10   9   8   7   6   5   4   3   2

Table of Contents

1.	**The Basics of DR DOS**..	**1**
1.1	Installing DR DOS..	5
1.2	The User Interface...	15
2.	**Storing Data**..	**25**
2.1	The Two Different Diskettes..	28
2.2	Formatting Floppy Diskettes..	32
2.3	Formatting A Hard Disk...	34
2.4	Checking Your Hard Disk..	36
3.	**DR DOS Shortcuts**...	**39**
3.1	DATE and TIME...	44
3.2	File Attributes..	47
3.3	Directories..	49
3.4	Organizing The Directory Structure...................................	54
3.5	The TREE Command...	55
3.6	Copying Entire Diskettes...	57
3.7	Wildcards..	60
3.8	Other Important Commands...	62
4.	**Backing Up Data**...	**65**
4.1	Performing Backup..	67
4.2	Restoring Data...	70
4.3	Partial Backups..	72
5.	**Filter Commands**...	**73**
5.1	Redirecting Data...	76
5.2	SORT...	78
5.3	MORE...	80
5.4	FIND...	81
6.	**ViewMAX**...	**83**
6.1	Starting ViewMAX...	86
6.2	Opening Files..	90
6.3	Menus and Commands...	91
6.4	Dialogs..	100
7.	**TaskMAX**...	**105**
7.1	Using TaskMAX..	112
8.	**DiskMAX**...	**115**
8.1	VDISK.SYS..	118
8.2	Super PC-Kwik Disk Cache...	119
8.3	DELWATCH...	121

8.4   DISKMAP...123
8.5   DISKOPT...124
8.6   SuperStor...127

9.   Memory Management.......................................**137**
9.1   Memory Areas..143
9.2   Displaying Memory...148
9.3   Starting The System.......................................150
9.4   HIDOS.SYS...152
9.5   EMM386.SYS..154
9.6   EMMXMA.SYS..156

10.   Special Utility Programs..................................**157**
10.1   EDITOR..159
10.2   PASSWORD..165
10.3   Security..168
10.4   FILELINK..172
10.5   TOUCH...178
10.6   CURSOR..179
10.7   DOSBOOK...180

11.   Fine Tuning DR DOS...**181**
11.1   CONFIG.SYS..183
11.2   The PATH Command..193
11.3   The APPEND Command..194
11.4   The Keyboard Layout.......................................195
11.5   The Environment Area......................................196
11.6   The System Prompt...198
11.7   Device Drivers..200

12.   Batch Files...**207**
12.1   Batch File Commands.......................................211
12.2   Modifying AUTOEXEC.BAT....................................214

13.   Error Messages..**217**
13.1   DR DOS Error Messages.....................................219
13.2   Error Situations..222

Appendices...**225**
A.   DR DOS vs. MS-DOS...227
B.   DR DOS Commands...233
C.   Glossary..238
D.   ASCII Table...246

Index...**249**

1. The Basics of DR DOS

1. The Basics of DR DOS

What is DR DOS?

Digital Research has developed a new operating system for PC users called DR DOS 6.0. In ordinary terms, DOS (Disk Operating System) handles the communication between you and the computer. You use DOS to tell the computer what you want it to do, and the applications programs use DOS to pass the information that it needs.

What is an Operating System?

An operating system is required to operate a PC. It controls and manages the devices like the screen, keyboard, mouse, printers and disk drives. It lets you communicate with your PC. This happens mainly through the screen, the keyboard and the mouse. The operating system also organizes and manages your computer's memory, diskettes, hard disk, the printer and the software.

DR DOS 6.0 Highlights

We'll discuss the features and advantages of using DR DOS throughout this book. In addition to the features in earlier versions of DR DOS and MS-DOS, the current version adds the following new features:

- DiskMAX™ for maximizing the speed and capacity of hard disk drives.

- TaskMAX™ providing an easy task switcher with textual cut and paste.

- Built-in security for protecting hardware and data.

- ViewMAX™ (an icon or graphical user interface).

- MemoryMAX™ optimizes memory management for 8086, 80286, 386, and 486 systems.

- Easy system optimization—undelete, unformat, extended utilities and system configuration tools.

Why Use DR DOS?

The help screens, screen editor and ViewMAX make DR DOS easier to use than MS-DOS.

If you're a network user, DR DOS may be your answer. An average network driver requires up to 128K bytes of RAM which is easily handled by DR DOS. Also, DR DOS has no affect on your applications.

If you're a laptop user, FILELINK is a very useful utility to quickly transfer files and data between two computers. For example, you can work on a laptop (with 3.5" diskettes) away from the office and transfer the files to your desktop PC (with 5.25" diskettes).

Why Use
This Book

Most of you would rather accomplish something productive rather than spend your time paging through a thick reference manual.

Maybe you're using an earlier version of MS-DOS and want to try the new features of DR DOS 6.0. You'll probably want to start using DR DOS as soon as possible.

There are many reasons for wanting to start quickly, all of them reason enough to get through this book and learn the necessities.

• In your daily work, you'll run into problems. We'll show you how to simply and quickly solve these problems, step by step.

• For most people, a solution is more important than theory. So we've kept theory to a minimum.

The statements at the margin of the page make it easy to find certain subjects. The pictures highlight practical tips and tricks. There is no simpler and quicker way to learn DR DOS.

1.1   Installing DR DOS

DR DOS is distributed on four diskettes in 5.25" format or 3.5" format.

We'll start out by explaining how to install DR DOS on a computer with a formatted hard disk but which does not have an operating system installed.

Starting
Installation

Installing DR DOS is easy. Your system configuration is automatically determined, and the selection of confusing options is eliminated. In fact, with other versions of DOS, installing and configuring for optimum memory usage is a time consuming trial-and-error process. DR DOS will configure your computer correctly to make the maximum amount of memory available for your applications.

Make a copy of your master DR DOS diskettes and always use these copies for installation. Use your DISKCOPY command, or another utility program which will copy the complete diskette. Start by inserting the first diskette into drive A: and switch on the computer. After the system starts, DR DOS displays a welcome message with some brief instructions about the installation process.

```
Welcome to the DR DOS Install program.

This program will install DR DOS either onto your hard disk, or
onto removable (floppy) diskettes.

HELP information is available on each option and edit field.
Press the <F1> function key while the option is highlighted,
or while the cursor is on the field.

You will be using:
      - the <Enter> key to select an option and move to the next screen,
        or finish editing a field
      - the cursor keys (UP and DOWN arrow keys and the <Tab> key),
        to move between options
      - the <Esc> key to return to the previous screen
      - the <F10> key to abort the Install Program and exit to DR DOS

      ▊ Press <Enter> to continue.
 <Screen> Printer
Save Current Screen in .PIX file
Insert diskette for drive B: and
   strike any key when ready
 <Enter>=continue  <F10>=abort
```

The DR DOS 6.0 Installation Welcome Message

Press Enter when you are ready to continue.

Preparing to Install DR DOS 6.0

The installation program needs to know if DR DOS 6.0 is to be installed on your hard disk or on a floppy diskette. Select either the hard disk or floppy diskette A: by pressing the arrow keys.

```
┌─────────────────────────────────────────────────────────────┐
│                                                               │
│       Welcome to the DR DOS Install program.                  │
│                                                               │
│                                                               │
│       Select the drive on which to install DR DOS:            │
│                                                               │
│       █ C: (DOS partition on hard disk)                       │
│                                                               │
│       ↔ A: (Floppy diskette drive)                            │
│                                                               │
│       Use the cursor keys to highlight the drive of your choice, │
│       then press <Enter> to confirm your selection.           │
│                                                               │
│                                                               │
│                                                               │
│                                                               │
│                                                               │
│ F1-Help  ↕-next/prev line  <Enter>-select option  <Esc>-prev screen  F10-abort │
└─────────────────────────────────────────────────────────────┘
```

Selecting the destination drive for installation

If the hard disk is not formatted, you are asked if the hard disk is to be prepared with FDISK. If your hard disk is already formatted, you can simply continue the installation process. If it is necessary to format your hard disk, refer to Section 2.3 (Formatting A Hard Disk).

Continue Installation

Press the (Enter) key to continue the installation process if your hard disk is correctly formatted. If you need to halt the installation process for any reason, just press the (F10) key.

If another version of DOS has been installed on your hard disk, the installation will save these files in case it is necessary to restore the original version of DOS at a later date. Also, if the AUTOEXEC.BAT and CONFIG.SYS files are already on your disk, the installation program will present an option to use the information in these files rather than create new files.

Generally, you will find it's best to allow DR DOS 6.0 to create new files, disregarding the information contained in the previous versions. This means it will be necessary to modify these files later to define paths and add any supplementary device drivers that might be needed.

```
╔══════════════════════════════════════════════════════════════╗
║                                                                ║
║        Welcome to the DR DOS Install program.                  ║
║                                                                ║
║                                                                ║
║        An AUTOEXEC.BAT file and a CONFIG.SYS file already exist on ║
║        the destination drive. If you wish the information contained ║
║        in these files will be used instead of the default values, ║
║        where applicable.                                        ║
║                                                                ║
║                                                                ║
║          ✧ Use the information in the existing file(s)          ║
║                                                                ║
║          ▮ Ignore the existing file(s)                          ║
║                                                                ║
║                                                                ║
║                                                                ║
║                                                                ║
║ F1=Help  ↕=next/prev line  <Enter>=select option  <Esc>=prev screen  F10=abort ║
╚══════════════════════════════════════════════════════════════╝
```

AUTOEXEC.BAT and CONFIG.SYS exist

Press Enter when you are ready to continue.

Memory Functionality

Now DR DOS will ask for information about configuring your memory. Three options are displayed on the screen.

```
╔══════════════════════════════════════════════════════════════╗
║                                                                ║
║        Welcome to the DR DOS Install program.                  ║
║                                                                ║
║                                                                ║
║        The default values of all the options in INSTALL can be set to ║
║        provide one of three memory/functionality combinations. Choose ║
║        the combination which matches your requirements.        ║
║                                                                ║
║                                                                ║
║          ✧ Maximum application memory at the expense of functionality. ║
║                                                                ║
║          ▮ Balance application memory and functionality.        ║
║                                                                ║
║          ✧ Maximum performance and functionality at the expense of ║
║            application memory.                                  ║
║                                                                ║
║                                                                ║
║ F1=Help  ↕=next/prev line  <Enter>=select option  <Esc>=prev screen  F10=abort ║
╚══════════════════════════════════════════════════════════════╝
```

Selecting the proper memory configuration

You need to select how to divide the memory between the operating system and the application area.

Selecting "Maximum application memory at the expense of functionality." allocates the maximum possible memory size for running applications, but sacrifices some system functionality.

The "Balance application memory and functionality." option is the best choice for most users. This will provide the best combination of functionality and memory usage.

You may want to achieve the best operating system performance, while sacrificing the amount of memory available for applications. Choose "Maximum performance and functionality at the expense of application memory."

When you have made your selection, press (Enter) to continue.

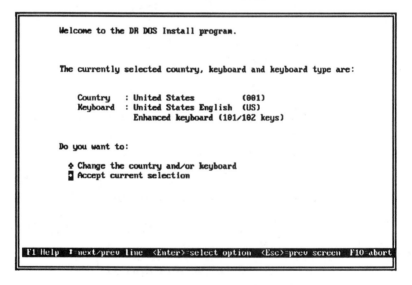

Country and keyboard settings

DR DOS displays the default country and keyboard settings and asks if the default settings should be accepted (the default setting may be already set for your own country). Pressing (Enter) will accept the current selection, or use the arrow key to select "Change the country and/or keyboard" and press (Enter) to display the optional country settings.

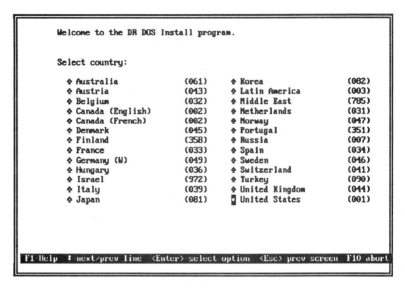

Country settings available with DR DOS 6.0

Select the proper configuration by using the arrow keys to highlight your choices, then press (Enter).

You may also specify the keyboard type as shown in the figure below.

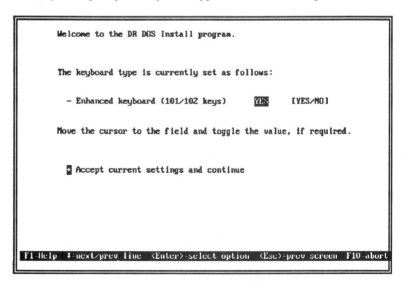

Select whether an enhanced keyboard type should be used

You may specify a directory for installing the DR DOS 6.0 files, or accept the default directory (DRDOS) by pressing (Enter).

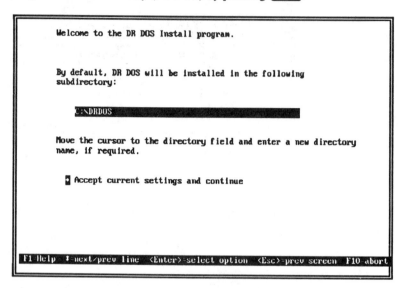

Selecting the directory for installing DR DOS 6.0 files on a hard disk

When the proper settings have been specified, the installation program is almost ready to begin copying files. But, before that can begin, you must decide whether to replace all copies of DOS files which have the same filename as a DR DOS file, or to leave them on the disk.

The installation program will search all directories on the disk and replace all copies. The default option is to replace all files with the same filename.

```
Welcome to the DR DOS Install program.


If required, the Install program will search all
the directories on the destination drive and replace all
copies of DOS files (i.e. any file with the same
filename as a DR DOS utility or driver).



  ✧ Do not replace all DOS files

  ▪ Replace all DOS files on the destination drive




F1-Help  ↕-next/prev line  <Enter>-select option  <Esc>-prev screen  F10-abort
```

Replace or skip duplicate filenames

At this point you can choose to skip the remainder of the configuration settings, accepting the default configuration, and continue with installing DR DOS 6.0.

```
Welcome to the DR DOS Install program.


At this point, you can skip the remainder of the configuration
procedure and proceed with the Installation. Defaults will be
used for the various system options and parameters.


NOTE: If you skip the configuration procedure any operating system
currently installed on your hard disk will be overwritten.





  ▪ Skip configuration and go directly to installation
  ✧ Proceed with configuration
F1-Help  ↕-next/prev line  <Enter>-select option  <Esc>-prev screen  F10-abort
```

You can skip the rest of the configuration process

11

Changes to your configuration are quite easy after installation is complete. Just run the SETUP command. These optional settings will be discussed later in this book.

Use the arrow keys to select "Proceed with configuration" and press Enter to continue the configuration process.

Pressing Enter to accept the defaults will cause any previously installed operating system to be overwritten. We recommend you make one more change to your configuration.

Additional configuration settings

Ignore all other settings for now and use the arrow key to highlight "Save Changes and Exit", the last menu option. Press Enter to continue.

You will be offered a chance to select whether to save the current operating system, or to overwrite all files. We recommend saving the old system. If you discover that essential software is incompatible with DR DOS 6.0 (a situation that DR DOS has promised will not occur with commercial software), you can use the UNINSTALL command to remove DR DOS and restore the previous operating system.

```
    Do you want INSTALL to save your old Operating System so that DR DOS
    can be successfully uninstalled?

    Do you want INSTALL to save your old Operating System so that DR DOS
    can be successfully uninstalled?


    ▮ YES - save old Operating System.

    ✦ NO  - do not save old Operating System.




 F1=Help  ↕=next/prev line  <Enter>=select option  <Esc>=prev screen  F10=abort
```

Save or overwrite old operating system

You can define the directory name for storing the old operating system
files, or select the default name supplied by DR DOS.

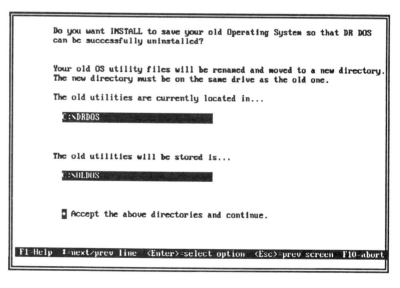

```
    Do you want INSTALL to save your old Operating System so that DR DOS
    can be successfully uninstalled?

    Your old OS utility files will be renamed and moved to a new directory.
    The new directory must be on the same drive as the old one.

    The old utilities are currently located in...
    C:\DRDOS


    The old utilities will be stored is...
    C:\OLDOS


    ▮ Accept the above directories and continue.

 F1=Help  ↕=next/prev line  <Enter>=select option  <Esc>=prev screen  F10=abort
```

Directory for old operating system

Enter a name or press (Enter) to continue.

Before continuing, the installation program will give you a chance to reconsider and make any necessary changes to your configuration settings.

```
       This concludes the configuration procedure.


       This concludes the configuration procedure.

       To review or change any of your choices, you can backtrack
       through the configuration screens using the <Esc> key.

       The Install Program will now copy the DR DOS system.




     █ Press <Enter> to continue.




  <Enter>=select option   <Esc>=prev screen   <F10>=abort
```

Configuration process completed

The remaining steps are automatic. Press (Enter) and follow the prompts to insert the proper diskettes to complete the installation.

Reboot   After installing DR DOS, restart your computer by pressing (Ctrl)+(Alt)+(Del).

1.2   The User Interface

After installing DR DOS 6.0 as explained in the previous section, reboot your computer by pressing Ctrl+Alt+Del, by pressing the reset button, or by switching off your computer then turning it back on.

As the computer boots, if your computer has a 286, 386, 386SX or 486 microprocessor, you may be asked whether you want to load the MemoryMAX software, while some versions of DR DOS 6.0 may automatically load MemoryMAX through the AUTOEXEC.BAT file. MemoryMAX will be explained in greater detail later in this book. For now, it's sufficient for you to know that it's a collection of device drivers and commands that are used for managing memory. The purpose of MemoryMAX is to give you more free memory for loading applications.

If DR DOS 6.0 prompts you about loading MemoryMAX, press Y to load the MemoryMAX software and continue with the booting process.

As your computer boots, you will see information similar to the following figure displayed on your screen. Don't worry if your messages are not exactly the same as these. By following the instructions previously given, the DR DOS 6.0 install program will have configured your computer for optimum usage.

After the booting process is complete, the system prompt will appear, and you are ready to begin working.

```
[DR DOS] C:\>
```

The default DR DOS system prompt

You can customize the system prompt to display the date and time or just about anything you want. This, too, will be explained in greater detail later in Section 11.6 (The System Prompt).

In general, the system prompt displays the drive identifier and the name of the current directory. For example:

```
[DR DOS] C:\>, C:\DRDOS or A:\
```

DR DOS system prompt

The blinking cursor shows the current cursor position in the input line. If you're experiencing difficulty seeing or distinguishing the cursor, you can change its appearance and flash interval. See Section 10.6 for information on the CURSOR command.

Editing
Functions

DR DOS even includes a command to simplify using the command line, especially for repetitive commands and command line editing. In order to use an extended command line editor, follow these steps to modify your CONFIG.SYS file.

Type:

```
EDITOR CONFIG.SYS  Enter
```

The DR DOS EDITOR will be loaded with your CONFIG.SYS file. Look through the CONFIG.SYS file listing for one of the following lines:

```
HISTORY=OFF
HISTORY=ON
```

If neither line exists, use the arrow keys to move the cursor to the last line in the file.

Now type:

```
HISTORY=ON  Enter
```

Your CONFIG.SYS file should look something like this:

```
       c:\config.sys  chr=1 col=1                                    ins.  ^J=help
SHELL=C:\COMMAND.COM C:\ /P /E:512
BREAK=ON
      strike any key when ready
FILES=20
FCBS=4,4
FASTOPEN=512
LASTDRIVE=E
COUNTRY=001,,C:\DRDOS\COUNTRY.SYS
HIDOS=ON
?"Load MemoryMAX software (Y/N) "DEVICE=C:\DRDOS\EMM386.SYS /F=AUTO /K=3328 /B=F
DEVICE=C:\SSTORDRV.SYS
HISTORY=ON
```

The CONFIG.SYS file modified to include the HISTORY command

After you have entered this line, press Ctrl+K X. This key combination will save the file and exit the EDITOR program. We'll examine the DR DOS Editor more thoroughly in Section 10.1 (EDITOR).

This activates the HISTORY command which stores commands in a memory buffer with the default size of 512 bytes. This size can be changed, as will be explained later. The buffer size can be set between 128 and 4096 bytes.

Now you can recall commands to reuse or edit. If you make a typing error when entering a command, you can easily redisplay the command, edit it and reissue it.

If HISTORY is ON, you can use expanded command line editing.

The HISTORY function can also be activated during installation or by using the SETUP command:

SETUP Enter

The welcome screen you saw during installation appears. Press Enter to continue. Your various configuration files are read and the memory allocation screen is displayed. Press Enter again to continue without making changes to the way memory is being used.

17

Next, the master configuration screen is displayed. Use the arrow keys to select "System Parameters," as shown below.

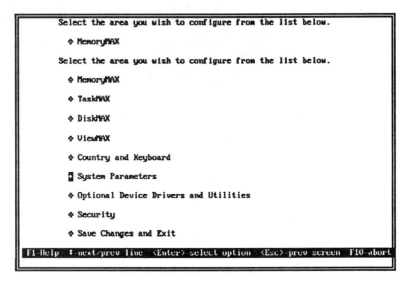

The SETUP configuration screen

When you press (Enter) to select "System Parameters," the following screen is displayed:

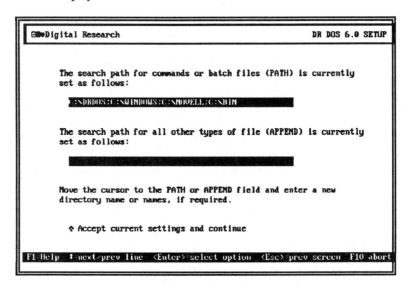

Defining DR DOS search paths

It's not necessary at this point to make changes to this screen, so press
[Enter] to continue.

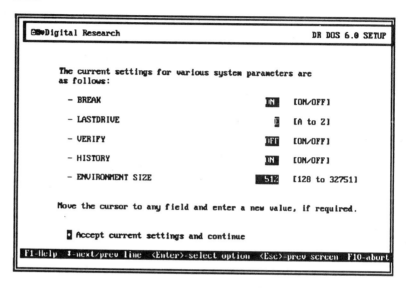

More system parameters

Although this screen is highly useful and provides a means of modifying
your system quite easily, we'll skip a detailed explanation for now and
cover it in depth later.

Use the arrow keys to select HISTORY, then press [Spacebar] to toggle
the HISTORY line ON or OFF. When you have set HISTORY, use the
arrow keys to select "Accept current changes and continue" and press
[Enter].

The next screen allows configuring the buffer size and enabling insert
mode for the HISTORY command.

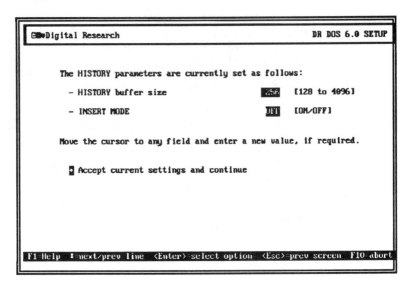

The HISTORY configuration screen

Continue pressing (Enter) until SETUP offers an exit to DOS or to reboot. Select the reboot option to install your changes. Your computer will reboot, and HISTORY will be installed.

Editing Keys The following standard editing keys can be used to edit command lines. For example, if you typed in the following command:

```
REMAME EXAMPLE.TXT SAMPLE.TXT (Enter)
```

DR DOS responds with:

```
Command or filename not recognized
```

Press the ⬆ arrow key to redisplay the command. Edit individual command lines with the ⬅ and ➡ arrow keys. Then use one of the following keys to move the cursor and edit the command:

Key	Command line edit function
F1	Copies and displays one character of the stored line.
F2	Copies all characters up to a specified character.
F3	Copies all remaining characters of the stored line.
F4	Deletes all characters up to a specified character.
F5	Copies the current line for editing (not as a command).
F6	Specifies the End-Of-File marker.
Ins	Switches between insert and overwrite modes.
Del	Deletes the current highlighted character.
Esc	Cancels the command line; characters are unchanged.
Backspace	Deletes the previous character.

In addition to the standard editing keys, HISTORY adds the following Extended Command line editing keys:

Key	HISTORY edit function
Enter	Enters the command line.
↑	Moves to the previous command.
↓	Moves to the next command.
→	Moves one character to the right.
←	Moves one character to the left.
Home	Moves the cursor to the beginning of the line.
End	Moves the cursor to the end of the line.
Ctrl+A	Moves the cursor one word to the left.
Ctrl+F	Moves the cursor one word to the right.
Ctrl+Y	Erases the line.
Ctrl+B	Erases all characters preceding the cursor.
Ctrl+K	Erases all characters from cursor to the end of the line.
Ctrl+T	Erases the rest of the word beneath the cursor.
Ctrl+−	Turns the search mode on and off. The default is off.
Ctrl+R	Starts the command line search.
Backspace	Deletes the character to the left of the cursor.
Del	Deletes the character at the cursor.
Ins	Switches between insert and overwrite modes.

Scroll Through Commands	HISTORY is not only available for editing commands typed incorrectly. After typing a command once, you can page through the individual command lines using the ⬆ and ⬇ arrow keys. Press the ⬆ arrow key to scroll backwards and press the ⬇ arrow key to scroll forwards.

For example, instead of typing a frequently used command such as:

`CD..` Enter

each time, Enter it once. Next time you need it, press the ⬆ and ⬇ arrow keys until that command appears next to the system prompt. Then press the Enter key. Remember that you must enter the command at least once and that you cannot exceed the memory buffer of HISTORY.

Internal and External Commands	DR DOS differentiates between internal and external commands. Internal commands are loaded into main memory when you start your computer. Since these commands reside in memory, they're available for you to use immediately. COPY, DEL and TYPE are examples of internal commands.

You'll use external commands (also called transient commands) less frequently than internal commands. These commands are loaded from the hard disk or diskette before they are executed and therefore save memory in your computer. CURSOR, FORMAT, TOUCH are examples of DR DOS external commands.

Help	Help is available for most of the external commands of DR DOS. A help screen provides valuable information concerning the command. This is a time saving advantage because it is not necessary to refer to manuals or other text.

You can see a help screen by typing the command name followed by the /H switch. For example, to display help information about using the TREE command, type the following:

`TREE /H` Enter

The exact syntax of the command and the valid parameters and switches are briefly described for you in this help information.

```
[DR DOS] C:\>tree /H
TREE R1.51    Show directory structure
    strike any key when ready Digital Research Inc. All rights reserved.

TREE [/Help]  [d:][path][filename[.ext]] [/B] [/F] [/G] [/P]

    d:            drive which tree is to search
    path          directory where search is to begin (default is root)
    filename.ext  file to find

    /B            brief mode - omit file totals
    /F            display all files
    /G            graphical directory display
    /P            pause after each page

Multiple files may be specified on the command line.

[DR DOS] C:\>
```

Help for the TREE command

2. Storing Data

2. Storing Data

When you switch off your PC, all the information which was stored in the memory of the PC is lost. Therefore, it's important to somehow save this information. Otherwise you would have to re-enter the information or program every time you want to use it. You can use numerous types of recording media and mass storage devices to store data. These include punch cards, magnetic tape, floppy disks and hard disks.

Disk Drives

The most common mass storage devices for PCs are disk drives. They vary in size, portability and in memory and access capacities.

Although there are many different types and styles of disk drives, they all have the same basic functions. They read data from and write to diskettes and send the data to the computer.

Floppy Disk Drives

Floppy disk drives and hard disks are the main types of disk drives which your PC can use. The first PCs had disk drives which would read/write on only one side of the diskette. The storage capacity of one of these disks was 180K. Although too small for most of today's applications, when you consider that the working memory of the first IBM PC was only 64K, a storage capacity of 180K was remarkably high.

The two different sizes of floppy diskettes you can use in a floppy disk drive are 5.25" and 3.5". See Section 2.1 for more information.

The advantage of using a floppy diskette (or simply diskette) is that it's very easy to exchange data with either the 3.5" and 5.25" diskettes. Since the diskette and the disk drive are two separate units, all you need to do is remove a diskette from one PC system and insert it into another PC system.

The disadvantage of using these diskettes are that the access time is too slow and the storage capacity is too small for many professional applications.

Hard Disks

Hard disks are usually mounted inside the computer case. A hard disk is the only choice for storing larger amounts of data. The average hard disk holds 20 megabytes (over 20 million characters or about 10,000 typewritten pages).

The disadvantages of hard disks are that disks cannot be exchanged, hard disks are more expensive and are sensitive to shock.

2.1 The Two Different Diskettes

Diskette
Sizes

As we mentioned earlier, there are currently two different sizes of diskettes: 3.5" diskettes and 5.25" diskettes. Both of these diskettes are double-sided, which means that data is stored on both sides of the diskette.

The main difference between the two sizes is in their storage capacities. The storage capacity for a 3.5" diskette ranges from 360K to 1.44Mb and the storage capacity ranges from 360K to 1.2Mb for a 5.25" diskette. The diskettes with the higher storage capacity are known as "high density" diskettes.

The actual storage capacity of a diskette is predetermined by the number of tracks and sectors during physical formatting (we'll discuss how to format a diskette in Section 2.2).

A track is one of several concentric rings encoded on a disk during the format process. The tracks allow the computer to store data at specific locations on the disk. The number of the track begins with 0 (from the outside edge) and increase as you move towards the center of the disk.

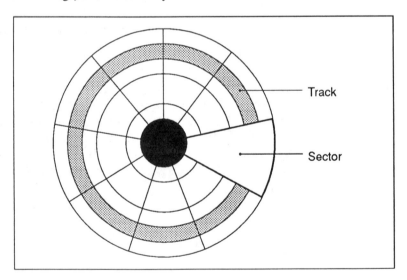

Floppy diskette tracks and sectors

The tracks are divided into sectors and, as a rule, consist of 9, 15 or 17 sectors. The sector is the area the computer uses to store data at specific locations on the disk for retrieval. Normal PC sectors contain 512K of usable area.

3.5" Diskette   The following picture shows the different parts of a 3.5" diskette:

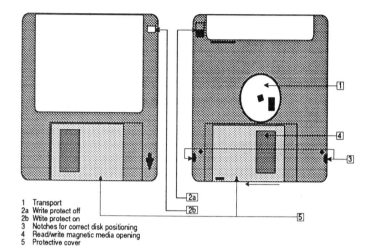

1   Transport
2a Write protect off
2b Write protect on
3   Notches for correct disk positioning
4   Read/write magnetic media opening
5   Protective cover

A 3.5" floppy diskette

The 3.5" diskette format has a total of 80 tracks. The diskettes with 720K are formatted with 9 sectors and the high density diskettes are formatted with 18 sectors. They have a capacity of 1.44Mb.

Handling 3.5"   When handling 3.5" diskettes, hold the disk so that the metal guard (#5
Diskettes   on the above picture) points away from you. Look for a metal circle (#1) built into one side of the disk. Position the disk so that this metal circle points toward the floor. Slide the disk into the drive so the protective cover enters the disk drive first. Gently slide the disk until it seems to stop. Give the disk a push until it locks firmly into place.

5.25" Diskette   The following illustration shows the different parts of a 5.25" diskette:

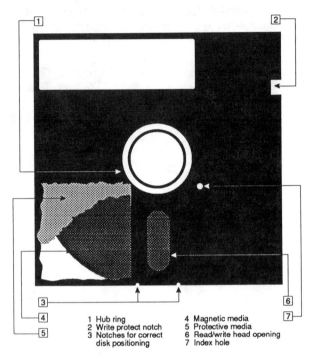

1 Hub ring	4 Magnetic media
2 Write protect notch	5 Protective media
3 Notches for correct	6 Read/write head opening
disk positioning	7 Index hole

A 5.25" floppy diskette

Handling 5.25"   When handling the 5.25" diskette, the write protect notch (#2 in the
Diskettes   above picture) should be to your left and the large opening (#6) that
exposes the magnetic material should be farthest from you.

Most system diskettes do not have a write protect notch. This is to
prevent you from accidently erasing the system disk. In this case,
position the disk so that the disk label points toward you and the opening
points away from you.

Make certain that the lever above the disk drive is parallel with the disk
opening (since your drive may be different, check your user manual).
Slide the disk into the topmost horizontal slot shiny material first, and
with the write protect notch to your left and the label toward you. Slide
the disk in until it stops. Move the lever 90° down so that it blocks the
disk drive slot. The PC cannot read the disk if the drive isn't closed.

The 5.25" diskettes are usually double density. This means that each side is divided into 40 tracks with 9 sectors per track. Since each sector has a capacity of 512 bytes, the capacity of the diskette is found with this formula:

```
2 sides * 40 tracks * 9 sectors * 512 bytes = 368,640 bytes
```

The same formula is used for higher density diskettes (HD or High Density) which have 80 tracks and 15 sectors per track. These diskettes have a capacity of 1.2Mb.

2.2   Formatting Floppy Diskettes

In this section we'll show you how to format diskettes. This is a process of preparing new disks to accept data. Before proceeding with this section, make sure you're using quality double-sided, double-density diskettes.

Why Format Diskettes?

Most new blank diskettes are not formatted so you must format them first before using them. It's more cost effective for the manufacturer to sell disks which you can format for your own computer system. Therefore, you must format each diskette before working in DR DOS. Formatting divides the diskette into tracks which are in turn subdivided into sectors.

Formatting a diskette also creates the following:

Boot record
> This is the first track (track 0) on the diskette and allows DR DOS to determine whether the diskette was prepared to operate under DR DOS and which format the diskette contains.

File Allocation Table (FAT)
> This portion of all DR DOS formatted diskettes contains information on the number and location of files and available storage space. It records used, unused and defective sectors of a diskette, as well as which sectors belong to a certain file.

Root directory
> This is the main (highest level) directory found on either a floppy diskette or a hard disk. This root directory can be accessed by entering the drive letter, the colon and a backslash. You can display the root directory of drive A: with the command:

```
DIR A:\  [Enter]
```

Formatting a diskette prepares it for use with DR DOS. You can reformat a diskette any number of times. However, formatting a diskette which is already formatted and contains data, will erase that data.

Type the following exactly as it appears below (don't press [Enter] yet):

```
FORMAT A:
```

Make sure that this is exactly what it says on your screen. Make any necessary corrections. Now press the [Enter] key. The screen displays this or a similar message:

```
Insert target diskette in drive A:
and press ENTER when ready...
```

Insert a blank, unformatted diskette in drive A: and press the (Enter) key. The screen may or may not display a message about its method of formatting a disk. Most 5.25" disks have tracks and sectors as mentioned earlier, while many 3.5" systems refer to heads and cylinders. You may also see the progress of the format on the screen. This information will appear below the format method previously discussed.

If the format is successful, the screen displays the following message:

```
Enter volume label (Max. 11 characters, ENTER for none)
```

Enter the volume label (diskette name) if one is desired, and press (Enter). Finally, the results of the format are displayed.

```
Disk formatted successfully

       362496 bytes total disk space.
       362496 bytes available on disk.

Format another diskette (Y/N)
```

If you don't need to format another diskette press (N). To format another diskette, press (Y), and the format process is repeated.

Although drive A: is handled as a 360K drive by default, you can format other types of diskettes. For example, you can format both 360K diskettes and 1.2Mb diskettes in a 1.2Mb drive. To format a 360K diskette in a 1.2Mb drive, type the following:

```
FORMAT A: /4 (Enter)
```

or

```
FORMAT A: /F:360 (Enter)
```

To format a 720K diskette in a 1.4Mb drive, type either of the following:

```
FORMAT A: /F:720 (Enter)
```

or

```
FORMAT A: /N:09/T:80 (Enter)
```

2.3 Formatting A Hard Disk

We briefly mentioned formatting a hard disk in Chapter 1 during the installation procedure of DR DOS. However, we did not mention dividing the hard disk into different partitions.

Installing the Hard Disk

As we mentioned in Chapter 1, some manufacturers perform low-level formats at the factory. You may want to see whether your hard disk has already been through low-level formatting. Use the FDISK utility:

```
FDISK [Enter]
```

If FDISK can read the drive and display information, the hard disk has undergone low-level formatting.

Low-level formatting is done either with a special program included in ROM on the hard disk controller card or with special formatting software like Speedstor® from Storage Dimensions or the DiskManager® from Ontrack. If you continually get read errors when using the hard disk, we recommend that you repeat the low-level formatting of the hard disk.

Dividing the Hard Disk

The next step in preparation of the hard disk is partitioning. A partition is a physical section of the hard disk separate from other sections. The DR DOS operating system considers each of these sections as a separate disk.

The partitioning is done with the FDISK utility program. FDISK can divide a hard disk into one primary partition (containing DR DOS) and one extended partition. If a hard disk is shared among several users you might consider partitioning it for each user.

The maximum size for the partition is 512Mb, although you can use smaller partitions.

Although DR DOS only requires the primary partition, you'll need to create an extended partition if you have additional space available on the same hard disk.

This extended partition is assigned the next logical drive letter (D: through Z:). For example, if your hard disk is 60Mb, you could create a primary partition of 32Mb and create an extended partition with 28Mb.

The extended partition can contain as many logical drives as you need.

```
FDISK R1.50 · Fixed Disk Maintenance Utility
Copyright (c) 1986,1988,1990 Digital Research Inc. All rights reserved.

Partitions on 1st hard disk (40.5 Mb, 976 cylinders):
No Drive Start End  MB   Status Type
 1   C:    0   975  40.4   A    DOS 3.31




Select options:
1) Create DOS partition
2) Delete DOS partition
3) Select bootable partition


Enter desired option: (ESC = exit) [?]
```

FDISK information display for a 40Mb single partition hard disk

A logical drive is a subdivision of a hard disk indicated by a specific letter. The first subdivision usually is designated as D because the primary partition is designated as C. Logical disk drives are treated like any other kind of disk drive. Each disk drive gets its own label and must be formatted.

You must specify at least one logical disk drive in the expanded partition so that you can separately address the hard disk partition. FDISK automatically displays this menu after you successfully create the extended partition.

Each of these partitions can use a different and an incompatible operating system. For example, DR DOS can manage one partition and UNIX can manage another partition.

Saving System Files   Using the FORMAT command with the "/S" switch copies required system files to the hard disk. Without these files you cannot start DR DOS from the hard disk. When using a hard disk, the FORMAT command prompts you before the actual formatting. This prompt asks if you really want to erase all of the data on the hard disk (which takes place during formatting).

35

2.4   Checking Your Hard Disk

Checking the
Hard Disk

Since the information on your disks is important, you obviously do not want to lose it. Therefore, it's a good idea to check the contents of your hard disk periodically. You probably have used the DIR command to display the contents of the hard disk. However, DR DOS offers another command for checking the contents of the hard disk and checking the hard disk for errors. This is the CHKDSK (short for CHecKDiSK) command.

CHKDSK reads all of the subdirectories and examines the allocation of sectors on the hard disk. CHKDSK will inform you of any errors it detects. The CHKDSK command looks at the memory usage and file status of the disk and your PC's memory usage.

Since CHKDSK is an external command, it must load from the hard disk:

CHKDSK (Enter)

Soon after the hard disk starts spinning, you'll see the following or similar information on your screen:

```
[DR DOS] C:\>chkdsk
Volume DRDOS60     created Aug-8-1991 10:58
   strike any key when ready
42,366,976 bytes total disk space.
   194,560 bytes in 10 hidden files.
    38,912 bytes in 15 directories.
16,599,040 bytes in 532 user files.
    28,672 bytes in 14 pending delete directories.
 7,751,680 bytes in 184 pending delete files.
17,754,112 bytes available on disk.

   655,360 total bytes of memory.
   594,688 total bytes of free memory.
   594,208 bytes in largest free memory block.

[DR DOS] C:\>
```

CHKDSK

You can use CHKDSK for several different purposes. For example, by using the "/F" switch you can have CHKDSK perform certain limited corrective measures. However, if you use this switch, we recommend backing up the contents of the hard disk to floppy diskettes. After you make backup diskettes, use the "/F" switch to attempt to repair the errors.

If you use CHKDSK without this switch, no corrective measures are performed to the hard disk.

Different ways exist for using CHKDSK on different disk systems. To demonstrate this, you'll need your BACKUP SYSTEM disk and the WORK1 disk for all the instructions below.

The FAT and the directories are the bookkeeping system of the hard disk and floppy diskettes. CHKDSK is used to check for "bookkeeping" errors.

Let's say that you're using an application program which has opened one or more files for writing. If the power to the computer is accidentally turned off, the file management information may not reflect the correct status of the files. In short, the File Allocation Table may not be in sync with the file.

CHKDSK spots small errors and problems before they become major problems and destroy data. A computer with its file management system out of sync can spend a long time waiting for nothing to happen. If, for example, data in a spreadsheet calculation disappears or the data from the previous day vanishes, there may be an error in the FAT or a directory.

Checking the Directory Initially, use CHKDSK without any switches. Using CHKDSK this way tells you if there are any potential errors.

CHKDSK can also be used with the /V switch. For example, type the following command:

```
CHKDSK /V  Enter
```

The /V switch (verbose) lists the complete path names for all of the files on the current drive and saves statistical information about that drive. This information is useful when trying to locate corrupted data on a disk.

As previously mentioned, CHKDSK will not correct any errors it detects unless you instruct it to do so by using the /F switch.

Using the /F switch instructs CHKDSK to write the corrections back to the disk. Since /F usually changes the File Allocation Table, some loss of data may occur. Therefore, you should back up your hard disk before using CHKDSK with the /F switch.

Since CHKDSK is one of the external DR DOS commands, you can use this command to check another disk drive. To check disk drive A:, insert a the diskette in drive A: and add the parameter "A:" to the standard CHKDSK command:

```
CHKDSK A: Enter
```

This command tells the computer to check the disk in drive A:.

We recommend that you perform this test on your hard disk and floppy diskettes on a regular basis. It is better to spend a small amount of time performing this task than to have a completely ruined disk.

Chapter 3 provides information on other commands, functions and instructions you can perform on your disk drive and hard disk.

3. DR DOS Shortcuts

3.   DR DOS Shortcuts

Any operating system spends most of its time managing files. Files can be categorized as either data files or program files. There is a difference between data files and program files. Program files contain a program that is used by the computer. Data files consist of data that are manipulated by programs (program files). For example, a word processing program is a program that creates or changes textual data.

DR DOS recognizes a program file by its name. A filename consists of two parts: the name and an optional extension. The filename is from one to eight characters long. The extension is from one to three characters long and is separated from the name by a period (.).

The following characters are allowed in filenames:

Letters	A to Z
Numbers	0 to 9
Special Characters	! # $ % ^ & () - _ ' {}

Starting Programs

DR DOS can only "run" or execute files which have an .EXE, .COM or .BAT extension. For example, if you type in "EDITOR" and press (Enter), DR DOS looks for the EDITOR file. A file is executed, if one exists, provided it has the specified name and one of these extensions: .EXE, .COM or .BAT. Files with other extensions are considered data files and cannot be executed by DR DOS.

The extension distinguishes files so that they can be arranged in certain categories.

Finding Files

DR DOS lets you read directories using the DIR command (the abbreviation for DIRectory). The DIR command displays the directory of the disk as listed in the system prompt.

Enter the following to display the directory:

```
DIR (Enter)
```

The filenames may move so fast that you cannot read them or find the desired filename until the directory stops moving. This movement is called scrolling because the information moves past as if you were rolling information on a scroll.

Your directory may look similar to the following:

```
Volume in drive C Does not have a label
Directory of C:\TEXT\BEGIN

.               <DIR>       3-21-91   1:42p
..              <DIR>       3-21-91
IMMO    STY     1024    4-22-89  12:02p
IMMO    BAK     91136   2-28-91  11:30p
IMMO    DOC     91136   7-28-91   4:46p
DOS     DOC     6144   12-22-90   8:31a
        6 File(s)      7225344 bytes free
```

Each program or set of data appears in the listing as follows:

The leftmost column displays the filename (the name of the program/data file).

The three-letter code following represents the file extension, indicating the type of file. .COM and .EXE files are executable (running) programs, while .DOC (DOCument) and .TXT (TeXT) files are usually readable text files.

The numbers represent the size of each file in bytes.

The last two entries in each line display the date and time that the file was last saved. Notice that all the above files were created or saved on the same date and that the time uses "a" to represent a.m. (morning) and "p" to represent p.m. (afternoon).

The Difference is Different Extensions

Note the three files named IMMO in the previous display. DR DOS can tell these files apart by their different extensions. The .DOC extension means that the file is a document file, the .BAK extension means that it's a backup file and the .STY extension means that it is a style sheet file.

These extensions for data files are assigned by an application. The above extensions are used by the word processing application Microsoft Word.

The first line that is displayed after the DIR command is executed says "Volume in drive C does not have a label." DR DOS manages files on disks that have certain names. A computer generally uses more than one disk drive. Usually one floppy drive and one hard disk are installed in a system. The floppy drive has the identifier "A:" and the hard disk has the identifier "C:".

In our case we are asking to see a list of files contained on drive C:. To display the files in drive A:, we must tell DR DOS by typing "DIR A:".

Here are other examples of the DIR command:

DIR /P	Displays the directory listing on the screen one page at a time.
DIR /W	Displays the directory listing in wide format. Directory names are preceded by backslashes.
DIR *.	Displays all entries that do not have extensions, such as subdirectories and files without extensions.
DIR *.COM	
	Displays only files that have the extension "COM".

3.1   DATE and TIME

Although you may not consider the date and the time as very important, each plays a larger role than may at first be apparent. Every time you change or create a file, your PC notes the data and time of the change or creation.

This allows you to view the filenames according to the data and time they were created or changed.

The date is set or checked with the DATE command and the time is set or checked with the TIME command.

Many computers feature a built-in clock. This eliminates the need to enter the time and date every time you turn on the computer.

Setting the Date

Enter the following to set or check the date:

```
DATE [Enter]
```

The following or similar message should appear on the screen:

```
Date Thu 2-23-91
Enter date (mm-dd-yy)
```

Notice the date structure. It appears in MM-DD-YY format. This means that to assign the current system date, you must enter the month as two digits (for example, April appears as 04), the day as two digits (for example, the sixteenth appears as 16) and the year as two digits (enter 1991 as 91).

Enter the following text exactly as it appears here. Separate each number with minus signs:

```
04-12-90 [Enter]
```

The computer displays the system prompt. It doesn't look like anything happened. Enter the following:

```
DATE [Enter]
```

Now the following appears on the screen:

```
Current date is Wed 8-14-91
Enter new date:
```

Press (Enter).

You can enter a new date in another way as well. Enter the following text, which makes the new date a parameter of the DATE command:

```
DATE 8-15-91 (Enter)
```

The computer displays the system prompt. Now when you enter the DATE command again, the computer responds:

```
Current date is Thu 8-15-91
Enter new date:
```

Press the (Enter) key.

Notice that months and days numbering less than 10 only require one digit. Also, notice that the year doesn't require the century. We just enter 91 or whatever year, and the PC assumes we're in the 1900s.

You can also show the day for any date in the years 1-1-1980 to 12-31-2099. Type the following:

```
DATE 1-1-2000 (Enter)
DATE (Enter)
```

The PC should say that the current date is Saturday, January 1, 2000. Any dates outside the accepted range will result in:

```
Invalid date
Enter new date:
```

Setting the Time

Setting or checking the time is very similar to setting the date.

Enter the following:

```
TIME (Enter)
```

The screen displays this or a similar message:

```
Current time is: 0:06:00:00
Enter new time:
```

Enter the current time in HH:MM:SS format. For example, enter the following to set the time to 10:00 a.m.:

```
TIME 10:00:00  (Enter)
```

Most computers today have built-in battery-powered clocks to keep constant track of the current time. The only time you'll normally need the date and time commands is when you adjust for Daylight Savings Time, or travel to a new time zone and need to adjust your computer to reflect the correct local time.

You can enter single digits as well. Entering the following for the time:

```
TIME 7:5:2<Enter>
```

Is read by the PC as:

```
07:05:02
```

If you enter illegal times like 26:00:00, the PC responds with the following or a similar message:

```
Invalid time
```

MS-DOS reads time in 24-hour format. For example, entering the following sets the time to 5:32 in the evening:

```
TIME 17:32:00<Enter>
```

Again, you must remember to press the (Enter) key at the end of input. This tells the PC to execute the command.

TOUCH   You can also use the TOUCH program to change the creation date and time of a file (see Chapter 10).

3.2   File Attributes

A file attribute is a hidden characteristic or code of a file. This code contains specific information on that file, and is stored with a file's directory.

An active attribute is set or switched on. If you reset an attribute, it's considered non-active or switched off.

DR DOS uses the following file attributes:

A	This is the archive attribute of a file. When the archive attribute (sometimes called the archive bit) is set, the file contents were changed since the last BACKUP command was performed. If the archive attribute is reset, then the file contents were not changed since the last BACKUP command. The BACKUP command resets the archive attribute as it performs its operation.
R	This indicates the file is a read-only file. If the read-only attribute is set, you cannot write to files or erase files set with the R attribute.
H	This attribute represents hidden. A file with this attribute set is called a hidden file. Hidden files do not appear in the file list when using the DIR command.
S	This attribute represents system. No normal DR DOS command can access any file when this attribute is set.

The ATTRIB command displays file attributes. Type the following:

ATTRIB (Enter)

This results in a display similar to the following, which shows us here that three files have the archive attribute set:

```
--a---          c:backup.log
------          c:cursor.txt
--a---           c:data.txt
--a---           c:data.bak
------          c:editor.bak
```

Changing
Attributes

You can change attributes using the ATTRIB command in the following manner: After typing the ATTRIB command, type the filename and the abbreviation for the attribute you want to change. Type a "+" in front of attributes you wish to set and a "-" in front of attributes you wish to reset. For example, if you want all files within the directory to have the R attribute, type the following:

ATTRIB *.* +R (Enter)

XDIR

The XDIR command displays an expanded directory. This command sorts files according to their names and displays the file attributes.

XDIR (Enter)

You can also use various command switches with XDIR. For example:

XDIR /P (Enter)

stops the XDIR command when the directory fills the screen. Press (Enter) to continue the XDIR command.

XDIR /S (Enter)

displays the files in subdirectories in the specified directory.

XDIR /T (Enter)

sorts the directory by time and date instead of alphabetically.

You can combine the switches:

XDIR /T /P (Enter)

The following shows a portion of the XDIR display:

```
DIRECTORY              7-04-91   10:35a   c:.
DIRECTORY              7-04-91   10:35a   c:.
--a---          530    7-02-91   10:53a   c:backup.log
------        1,024    7-22-91    4:53a   c:cursor.bak
------        1.536    7-22-91    5:05p   c:cursor.txt


..

--a---        7,680    7-22-91    1:41a   c:data.bak
--a---        6,144    7-08-91   10.29a   c:viewmax.bak
--a---        6,144    7-22-91   12:28p   c:viewmax.txt
total files 32    total bytes 273,908    disk free space 9,144,320
```

3.3 Directories

Directory
Structure

The best way to explain hierarchical file structure (HFS) is to give you some illustrations of how it works. If you don't have a hard disk, you may be tempted to skip this section but we recommend that you read through it. This is especially true if your PC or compatible uses 3.5" disk drives. You can also organize the memory capacity of that disk format by using HFS.

Since a hard disk can generally store hundreds and even thousands of files, there needs to be a way to organize the contents. DR DOS organizes these files by using a structure called the directory. A hard disk can be divided into a tree structure containing different areas stemming from the root directory. This division is done purely logically and not physically. No physical data area is reserved for the contents of a directory. A directory is managed by DR DOS in the same manner as a file.

Managing
Directories

A directory is created using the MD command. This is an abbreviation for MKDIR or "make directory". Type the following at the system prompt:

MD EXAMPLE (Enter)

Now type the DIR command to view the directory of your PC.

At first it seems like DR DOS has created a new file using the MD command. However, no file size appears after EXAMPLE. Instead, <DIR> appears in place of the number of bytes.

Next, type in the following:

DIR EXAMPLE (Enter)

If EXAMPLE was the name of a file, DR DOS would list the name, size and creation/most recent access date for the file. Instead, DR DOS displays two lines (one line has one dot and the second line has two dots), the word <DIR> and the date and time:

```
Volume in drive C is DIR_WORK
Directory of C:\EXAMPLE

.              <DIR>        3-09-87   3:23p
..             <DIR>        3-09-87   3:23p
        2 File(s)   7176192 bytes free
```

We need to change the EXAMPLE directory so it becomes the current directory. A directory is declared as the current directory by using the CD command, which stands for CHDIR or "CHange DIRectory".

Type in the following:

CD EXAMPLE (Enter)

Unless we explicitly specify otherwise, all of the commands that we discuss or show refer to the current directory.

To get out of the EXAMPLE directory, type the following exactly as it appears here:

CD .. (Enter)

Now when you enter a DIR command the screen displays all the directory names. The two periods tell DR DOS that you want to move up by one level in the directory. Moving up by levels brings you closer to the root directory (main directory).

Root Directory   You may wonder how to specify which directory you want. When in the root directory, you specify the name of the directory to which you want to move (EXAMPLE in the case above). To move back to the previous level, type the following:

CD .. (Enter)

Unless you seldom write and receive letters, you probably wouldn't keep your letters in desk drawers. You'll find that desk drawers stay organized if you use folders to hold your letters. That way, you can keep letters to each person in their own folders. The folders help you easily find these letters.

DR DOS allows you to keep directories within directories. The entries "." and ".." allow you to manage subdirectories. You've probably seen these entries when you type the DIR command.

The name of the highest directory in which the current directory is entered as a subdirectory is abbreviated with two periods (..). You can use the two periods (..) as an abbreviation for the path of the directory directly above the current directory.

For example, to display the root directory of the highest directory, type the following:

```
DIR .. Enter
```

Or to change to the highest level directory, type:

```
CD .. Enter
```

Copying Between Sub-directories

To copy files from one subdirectory into one which is the subdirectory of the highest directory of the current directory, type the following command:

```
XCOPY *.* ..\UNDER2 Enter
```

This method is useful when writing batch files because batch files do not have to depend on directory names.

Removing a Directory

The RD command (also called RMDIR—both are abbreviations for ReMove DIRectory) deletes an *empty* directory from memory. Type the following:

```
RD EXAMPLE Enter
```

The screen displays the following or a similar message:

```
Invalid directory specified
```

This message means that either the path is wrong or the name is not a directory.

If the following message is displayed, the directory is not empty:

```
Directory not empty or in use
```

First delete any files and additional directories then delete the directory itself.

Deleting Files

The DEL command is used to erase (or DELete) files. Type the name of the file you want to delete following the command name:

```
DEL filename Enter
```

51

DR DOS then searches for this file in the current directory. After the command is executed, the DR DOS prompt appears without any other messages. The file is now deleted.

You can also delete multiple files in one operation or you can delete files in other directories or drives.

Here are some examples:

DEL LETTER.TXT	Deletes the file LETTER.TXT from the current directory.
DEL \TEXTS\LETTER.TXT	Erases the file LETTER.TXT from the subdirectory called TEXTS.
DEL A:TEXTS.TXT	Erases the file TEXTS.TXT from the current directory on drive A:.
DEL *.TXT	Erases all files with the .TXT extension from the current directory.
DEL *.*	Erases all files in the current directory.
DEL A:\TEXTS	Erases all files in the TEXTS directory on drive A:.

The DR DOS operating system provides you with several different ways to organize the contents of a disk. Since a computer uses files, the organization of all disks revolves around the file. The file is the central object around which the entire structure is built. DR DOS creates the boot record, the FAT (File Allocation Table) and the root directory when formatting a diskette. File entries or subdirectories can be placed into the root directory after the formatting is complete.

How Many Files are Allowed in a Directory?

The number of file entries and subdirectory entries is limited only by the capacity of the root directory. The root directory of a hard disk can usually have 512 entries. On a floppy diskette there is a limit of 64 or 128 entries (depending on the storage capacity of the diskette). If you attempt to put more entries into the root directory, DR DOS will respond with a corresponding error message.

This error may be misleading because the storage media may have plenty of room for files but no room for file entries.

When you create a subdirectory with the MD or MKDIR command, the name of the subdirectory is registered in the field of the filenames. This sets bit 4 in the file attribute and labels the entry as a subdirectory. The directory creation date and time are also set.

A cluster is a memory area on the diskette that consists of four sectors on the hard disk. A cluster on the hard disk is 2048 bytes long. A subdirectory entry is 32 bytes long, so a single cluster can store approximately 64 entries. A second cluster is required if more than 64 entries are used. This second cluster must have room to store an additional 64 entries.

The read head of the hard disk must then travel to the track of the new cluster. This movement requires time. When many files are saved in a single subdirectory, the read head must be moved often. This may cause it to take more time to open a file than the actual processing of the data takes. Subdirectories can be made up of many file entries, but it is advisable to break up a large subdirectory into multiple smaller subdirectories.

3.4 Organizing The Directory Structure

One way to organize your hard disk is to limit the number of entries in the root directory. You can do this by putting only subdirectories in the root directory. Besides the subdirectory entries, some system files of DR DOS require you to place some files in the root directory. (Actually DR DOS requires that some system files be located in the root directory as well.) Then you can create a subdirectory for each of your applications.

For example, you can create a subdirectory for spreadsheets, for word processing, for desktop publishing, for telecommunications and so on. Then you can set up a PATH command to search the subdirectories for the executable files for the different applications.

Logically Dividing Files To maintain even more order, you can create separate subdirectories for programs and data. For example, you can place the program files of a word processor in one directory and the text or document files created by the word processor in another directory.

The directory that contains the programs of the word processor should be included in the PATH command of the AUTOEXEC.BAT file so that the word processor can be executed from any directory. The data for the word processor can be placed in different subdirectories according to their type (for example, letters, legal briefs, press releases, etc.). These subdirectories then contain data of the same type and to help you remember the contents of each subdirectory.

These types of subdirectories are easier to understand than subdirectories that have both programs and data mixed together.

3.5 The TREE Command

The following diagram shows a simple data tree on a hard disk:

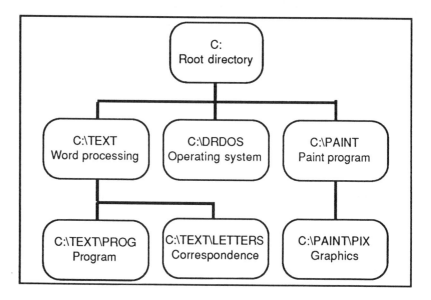

It's very difficult to remember all of this information, especially if you have several files on your hard disk. The DR DOS TREE command helps you visualize the contents of your hard disk. It displays not only the filename but also the number of bytes, files and the path.

You can use the following switches with the TREE command:

/F	The directory and filenames are listed.
/G	Graphically displays structure of the hard disk or the directory.
/H	Lists the help page.
/P	The output is shown page by page.
/B	A short list is shown.

The following picture displays the directory if you type the following:

TREE /G [Enter]

```
[DR DOS] C:\>tree /g
       bytes  files  path
     455,517     24  c:\
   2,473,422    104  √fffdrdos
           0      0  ≥   √ffftmp
          30      1  ≥   iffftemp
   2,451,396     64  √fffbin
      95,788      4  √fffmouse1
      75,765      3  √fffdos
      16,400      8  √ffftig
     543,057     42  √fffhijaak1
     375,079     13  √fffnovell
   3,104,524     71  √fffwindows
   1,772,951     44  ≥   √fffsystem
           0      0  ≥   iffftemp
   1,262,086     63  ifffoldos
total files 441    total bytes 12,626,015

[DR DOS] C:\>
```

Display of the results of the TREE /G command

If you type TREE without any switches, the display starts with the root directory. If you add the name of a directory, the display starts at that node of the directory structure.

3.6　Copying Entire Diskettes

Before you can copy a diskette, you must first format a target diskette (see Section 2.2). When copying data from one disk to another, the disk being copied is the source diskette and the target diskette is the diskette receiving data.

*COPY and
XCOPY*

You can copy diskettes using one of the following methods. The first method, using COPY and XCOPY, can be used if there are no "hidden files" on the diskette. DR DOS protects some system files by hiding them on the diskette. For example, if you copy a DR DOS installation diskette using this method, the copy will be incomplete because it contains hidden files. You'll need to use the DISKCOPY command instead.

You'll probably use the XCOPY (extended copy) command more than the COPY command since it has more options and is more powerful.

You can use XCOPY to copy all subdirectories, sub-subdirectories, password-protected files (although you will be prompted for the password) and you can rename files while copying them. There are a number of switches for the XCOPY command:

/H	Displays help text.
/A	Copies only files whose archive bit is set and does not change the archive bit.
/D:*date*	Copies only files whose *date* is identical to or later than the one given.
/E	Creates an empty subdirectory on the target drive.
/H	Includes hidden or system files.
/L	Copies disk label from one diskette to another as well as the specified files.
/M	Copies only files whose archive bit is set, then resets the archive bit.
/P or /C	Requires you to confirm the copying of each file.
/R	Overwrites files whose attribute is set to "read only".
/S	Copies files in subdirectories and in the source directory.
/V	Verifies the copy operation.
/W	Waits for a diskette to be inserted before starting the copy operation.

57

For example, the following use of XCOPY copies all files, directories and subdirectories from the hard disk to drive A: and verifies the copied files:

```
XCOPY C:*.* A: /E /S /V
```

COPY and XCOPY using two floppy disk drives

Make certain that the target diskette is formatted and place it in drive B:. Then place the source diskette in drive A:.

Type the following command:

```
COPY A:*.* B: Enter
```

This method, however, will not work if there are subdirectories on the source diskette. A subdirectory is a directory listed inside another directory. If this is the case, then use the XCOPY command instead.

The XCOPY command has an "/S" switch which copies the contents of all of the directories. To make a copy of the diskette contained in drive A: type the following:

```
XCOPY A: B: /S Enter
```

COPY and XCOPY on one floppy and one hard disk

Make a subdirectory on the hard disk and then copy the source files to this subdirectory:

```
MD C:\COPIES
XCOPY A:*.* C:\COPIES
```

Next, insert the source diskette in drive A: and type the following commands:

```
XCOPY C:\COPIES\*.* A:
DEL C:\COPIES
RD C:\COPIES
```

The last two commands erase the files from the hard disk and remove the subdirectory.

DISKCOPY   If you suspect hidden files are on the diskette, then use the DISKCOPY command. By using the DR DOS DISKCOPY command you can copy all files of a source diskette, including hidden files and files in subdirectories. You do not even need to format the target diskette since DISKCOPY formats it as it copies.

However, do not use DISKCOPY with a hard disk because this command erases the contents of the destination disk.

DISKCOPY using two floppy disk drives

If you're using two disk drives, make certain both drives are the same physical format. For example, a 360K 5.25" drive cannot be used to copy a 720K 3.5" diskette.

Insert the source diskette in drive A:. Then type the following command:

```
DISKCOPY A: B: Enter
```

DISKCOPY using one floppy disk drive

Another advantage of the DISKCOPY command is if you have only one floppy drive of the same physical size (e.g. one 360K 5.25" drive). DISKCOPY lets you make a duplicate using this single drive. For example, you can type:

```
DISKCOPY A: A: Enter
```

and the source diskette in drive A: is copied. You'll be prompted to exchange source diskettes and target diskettes (swap) as DISKCOPY proceeds. It's not as fast as having two drives, but it's less expensive.

3.7 Wildcards

Copying with
Wildcards

You can use wildcards when copying, deleting, renaming and performing other work with files. A wildcard is a character which represents another character or even a group of characters.

DR DOS offers two wildcards: the * character and the ? character. You can substitute the * character in place of one or more characters in the filename or extension or both. For example, to see a directory of filenames with the .EXE extension, type the following:

```
DIR *.EXE  Enter
```

You can use the ? wildcard to replace single characters in filenames and extensions.

For example, if you were to type the following:

```
DIR M?YER.TXT  Enter
```

DR DOS would locate files such as MAYER.TXT and MEYER.TXT, because DR DOS reads the question mark as any character.

Renaming
Files Using
Wildcards

The asterisk wildcard works with the RENAME command as well as the COPY command:

For example, you can rename several files with a .TXT extension so that they have extensions of .BAK (short for BAcKup). Type the following:

```
RENAME EXAMPLE*.TXT LETTER*.BAK  Enter
```

Then display a directory using the DIR command to confirm the change.

You can also rename files so that they have an extension. For example, to rename a file NOEXTEN to a .TXT extension:

```
RENAME NOEXTEN* NOEXTEN*.TXT  Enter
```

Deleting Files Using Wildcards

You can use the DEL command with asterisk wildcards to delete multiple files on a disk. However, you could delete files you don't want deleted if you are not careful.

Type the following but don't press the (Enter) key yet:

```
DEL *.*
```

Before pressing the (Enter) key, think of what you're about to do. The asterisks replace any combination of letters and numbers. This means that if you press the (Enter) key with a disk in the drive, DEL *.* deletes **everything** on the disk or in the directory.

Ask yourself if you really want to delete all the files on the disk. Is this the correct disk? If you want to proceed, press the (Enter) key.

DR DOS displays the following or a similar message on the screen:

```
Are you sure? (Y/N)
```

Press (Y) (Enter) to delete all the files.

The following is a list of file extensions which you should be very careful not to confuse. One typing error could destroy some very important data. This list contains the most frequently seen extensions but is by no means complete:

.BAK	Backup copy of a file
.BAS	Program in the computer language BASIC
.BAT	Batch file (We'll discuss batch files in Chapter 12)
.COM	Command (program) file
.EXE	Executable (program) file
.DOC	Document file, usually used with Microsoft Word
.TXT	Text files, normally used in word processing

3.8   Other Important Commands

Since subdirectories play a major roll in the management of files, many of the DR DOS commands deal with the processing of directories. Here are a few of these lesser used commands.

Determining a
Search Path

When DR DOS searches for executable program files (files containing .BAT, .COM and .EXE extensions) it searches for them in the directories specified by the most recent PATH command.

APPEND

An equivalent command for nonexecutable program files is the APPEND command. This command determines the search path for data files. Under normal circumstances DR DOS searches only the current directory for data files. APPEND tells DR DOS to look in other directories for data files.

If you have created a style sheet using a word processor and must use these style sheets often, you can place all of these style sheets into one specific directory. These style sheets seldom change and it doesn't matter from which directory you load them.

You can place the filled out style sheets in a special directory (called, for example, C:\FORMS\STYLES) and back them up from time to time. Then you can erase any unneeded style sheets.

The directory in which you will store the completed forms is called "C:\FORMS". When you want to fill in a template, type the following:

```
CD C:\FORMS  (Enter)
```

to switch to the directory where you saved the completed forms. Enter the directory as "C:\FORMS\STYLES" using the APPEND command. Then call the word processor and load the style sheet that you need.

When you see the root directory of the current directory in your word processor, you will not see the form style sheet because the APPEND command did not change the directory. Now you can fill in the form style. It is saved automatically in the "C:\FORMS" directory.

When you exit the word processor, don't forget to erase the search path for APPEND. If you fail to erase the search path, DR DOS will not know from which directory files are being read. We'll discuss how to erase the search path shortly.

The steps can automatically be executed in a batch file. If you call the EDITOR and name your form style sheet "FORM1", the batch file might look like this:

```
CD C:\FORMS
APPEND /X C:\FORMS\STYLES
EDITOR %1
APPEND ;
CD C:\
```

Erasing the Search Path

If this batch file is saved under the name "FORMS.BAT" you can tell the EDITOR to load the correct formula with the command "FORMS FORM1".

In our example we assumed that you had named the directory in which EDITOR was saved in the PATH instruction. This makes it possible to call EDITOR from any directory.

Then we used the APPEND command in two forms: First we used the "/X" option so that DR DOS searches the current directory for data files. We specified only one path with this command, but we could have used an entire row of paths (separated by semicolons). Next, we entered only one semicolon. This erases the search path for the APPEND instruction.

The above example illustrated a strategy that you should use: changes to system parameters should be reset when their task is done. Settings made with the APPEND command are only temporary and are connected to a certain task.

A second feature of this batch job is that it switches back to the root directory of hard disk C when the command is completed. If you write all of your batch jobs so that the system is in a certain condition at the end, you can avoid many errors because you'll use the same method. You can also place all batch files in a certain directory, for example the BAT directory, and insert this directory into the PATH instruction.

Assigning a Path to a Disk Drive

It is possible to assign a path to a drive label with the JOIN command. This is useful if you have divided the hard disk into partitions or are using multiple hard disks in the system. The JOIN command can assign hard disk D: a path in the root directory of hard disk C:. The entire hard disk D: is then a directory on C: and is then logically a part of drive C:. This method is specifically recommended on hard disks that have more than one partition.

Assigning a Drive Label to a Path

The reverse of JOIN is also possible. You can assign a drive label to a path using the SUBST command. This command can also assign a fixed drive to an existing path. This is useful when it is easier to give a drive label instead of a long pathname.

Condensing Long Path Statements

For example, instead of using a long pathname such as "C:\TEXTS\LETTERS\PRIVATE", it's easier to assign a fixed drive P: to this path with "SUBST P: C:\TEXTS\LETTERS\PRIVATE". Then in the future all you have to type is "P:".

Replacing a pathname with a drive label is useful in applications in which you can enter just a drive label and not a path. To make this command useful, you must use the LASTDRIVE command in the CONFIG.SYS file.

DR DOS normally only recognizes five disk drives (A: through E:). A management structure is created for each drive, so only create as many drive labels with LASTDRIVE as you will use.

For our example we must write the line "LASTDRIVE = P" in the CONFIG.SYS file so the drives A: through P: are available for use. The assignment of a drive label is cancelled by using the SUBST command with the option /D. The assignment of our example is cancelled with the command "SUBST P:/D".

4. Backing Up Data

4. Backing Up Data

To safeguard the data and programs on your hard disk, you should backup data to floppy diskettes frequently. While this is not a fun task and often requires a long time to do, it's highly recommended since your computer could malfunction, or a program could inadvertently destroy important information on your hard disk.

The DR DOS BACKUP and RESTORE are compatible with the data backup programs of MS-DOS Version 3.3. This is important information if you want to restore backups from MS-DOS onto your DR DOS system or vice versa.

4.1   Performing BACKUP

BACKUP can be used to backup an entire hard disk or diskette, individual directories, groups of files, or even single files.

Caution!   Files protected with a password are *not* backed up, unless the global password is set before running BACKUP, and the files have been protected with the same password. Refer to Section 10.2 for more information on using password protection.

Determining   Before backing up an entire hard disk, you should determine the number
Diskette Needs   of diskettes you'll need so that you have them available. To determine the number of diskettes needed, use the CHKDSK command discussed in Section 2.4.

You'll also need to know the storage capacity of the disk drive to which you're backing up the hard disk. CHKDSK will determine the number of bytes used on the disk. Divide this total by the capacity of the floppy disk drive. See Section 2.4 for more information about CHKDSK.

For example, if your hard disk has 17,000,000 bytes used and you're using a disk drive with a capacity of 720,000 bytes, then you'll need 17,000,000 / 720,000 = 23.6, or about 24 diskettes.

BACKUP   The advantage of using BACKUP over COPY is that BACKUP preserves
the structure of the directory hierarchy. The subdirectories are
automatically recreated by RESTORE as needed. All files which are
backed up with BACKUP must be restored using the RESTORE
command. We'll discuss RESTORE in Section 4.2.

You do not need to format the diskettes before running BACKUP. It
recognizes whether a diskette is already formatted. If the diskette is not
formatted, BACKUP will automatically format it. However, you can save
time backing up your data if the diskettes are already formatted.

During BACKUP the program prompts you to insert and change
diskettes. BACKUP displays the diskette number on the screen. Label the
diskette with this number. The diskettes must be inserted in the same
order to RESTORE the files. Example:

```
BACKUP C:\ A: /S/L Enter
```

This command saves the entire hard disk C:, including all subdirectories,
onto the diskettes in drive A: and places the log file BACKUP.LOG in
the root directory of the hard disk.

```
BACKUP D:\DOC A: Enter
```

This command makes a backup of the files in the DOC subdirectory on
the hard disk D: onto the diskettes in drive A:.

BACKUP /? or /H	Displays help screen.
BACKUP /S	Saves all files in the subdirectory of the given path.
BACKUP /M	Saves only files that were changed since the time of the last backup.
BACKUP /A	All of the files that are contained on the backup diskette remain untouched. The backup adds to the contents of the diskette. If this switch is not used, the backup erases all of the files on the backup diskette.
BACKUP /L:file	A protocol file is placed in the root directory of the source drive. The date, the diskette number and the data saved can be noted in this file each time something is saved. If you do not enter a filename with this option, the name BACKUP.LOG is automatically used.
BACKUP /F	Formats the target diskette before copying files. This is done automatically if the diskette has not been formatted.
BACKUP /D:date	Copies only the files that have been modified since a specified date.
BACKUP /T:time	Copies only the files that have been modified since the specified time.

When the copy is completed, BACKUP returns the following values to a batch file. You can test this batch file with an IF ERRORLEVEL statement:

Code	Meaning
0	No error during BACKUP.
1	BACKUP found no files to copy.
2	BACKUP could not copy some files due to a file sharing conflict.
3	User terminated procedure.
4	BACKUP ended by an error.

Do not use BACKUP if you have redirected a drive with the JOIN, SUBST or ASSIGN commands.

4.2   Restoring Data

RESTORE copies files which were backed up with the DR DOS BACKUP command. You can use RESTORE only on files which you performed a BACKUP.

The files are copied into the same directory from which they were backed up. You cannot RESTORE a file to a different directory.

Let's say you've previously backed up the entire hard disk C: using this command:

```
BACKUP C:\ A: /S/L
```

Now to write the files back onto the hard disk, use the following:

```
RESTORE A: C:\ /S
```

This command says that all of the files from the backup set, whose first diskette is in drive A:, should be returned to the hard disk.

This command will restore any files or subdirectories that were originally backed up, whether it was a single file, a single directory or a complete hard disk.

As a second example, say you've backed up the TEXTS subdirectory from drive D: using the command:

```
BACKUP D:\DOC A:
```

To restore these files from the backup diskettes, use this command:

```
RESTORE A: D:\ /S
```

In this example the "/S" switch tells RESTORE to include all of the files from subdirectories in the operation which are associated with the current directory. If you are unsure which files were restored from the diskette, you can use the "/R" switch instead.

The "/R" switch displays a report of which files would have been restored without actually performing the operation.

```
RESTORE A: D:\ /S/R
```

This command shows you which files would be restored to hard disk D:.

RESTORE /? or /H	Displays help screen.
RESTORE /S	Restores subdirectories associated with the current directory, creating required subdirectories as needed.
RESTORE /P	Prompts before restoring read-only files, or files that have changed since last backup.
RESTORE /A:date	Restores files that have been altered on the original disk on or after the date specified.
RESTORE /B:date	Restores files that have been altered on the original disk on or before the date specified.
RESTORE /E:time	Restores all files that have been altered on the original disk earlier than the time specified.
RESTORE /L:time	Restores all files that have been altered on the original disk later than the time specified.
RESTORE /M	Restores all files that have been altered on the original disk or deleted since the backup was done.
RESTORE /N	Restores all nonexistent files to the destination disk.
RESTORE /R	Reports which files would be restored without taking any action.

When completed with its tasks, RESTORE returns the following values to a batch file. You can test this batch file with an IF ERRORLEVEL statement:

Code	Meaning
0	No error during RESTORE.
1	RESTORE found no files to restore.
2	RESTORE could not restore some files due to a sharing conflict.
3	User terminated restore procedure.
4	Restoration process ended with an error.

Do not use RESTORE if you have redirected a drive with the JOIN, SUBST or ASSIGN commands.

4.3   Partial Backups

You may discover that saving an entire hard disk usually takes a large amount of time. Since backing up a large hard disk could take several hours, you should structure the hard disk using directories. Therefore, the number of files that need backing up is kept to a minimum.

Saving Individual Files

Let's say, for example, at the end of a week, it's only necessary to save the data files created using the word processor during the week. All of the files that belong to DR DOS are on the operating system diskette and the corresponding backup and don't need to be copied again. You can use the "/M" switch and backup only those files that were changed.

Save data and programs in different directories. Use the PATH instruction to set the command path so that important applications can be called from any directory. Create a separate directory for every project or subject and place all files together that logically correspond to each other. Then backup each directory or subdirectory on a separate set of diskettes.

Smaller Backups Are Quicker

It's also better to perform several small backup operations than one large backup. The method for saving files recommended above may require 60 or 80 diskettes instead of 40, but it allows you greater flexibility. You can quickly backup a directory onto three or four diskettes and then erase them from the hard disk if you need the space.

You no longer need to keep all relevant data together on the hard disk. Instead, you can use the hard disk more as "work memory" rather than a large "data memory".

If you use diskettes with a higher capacity, there is another type of partial backup. It's often possible to copy an entire directory onto one diskette by using the higher capacity of the high density diskettes. If that is the case you can simply work with the COPY or XCOPY command.

5. Filter Commands

5. Filter Commands

There are occasions when it's easier to use the output from one program as the input for another program. A filter command in DR DOS can read data from one file, change or reduce the input and write the filtered data into a second file.

The current standard input device is used as the input file and the current standard output device is used as the output file. The standard input device is usually the keyboard and the standard output device is usually the monitor. This makes it possible to link multiple filters behind each other and filter data repeatedly in one operation.

For example, if you have so many directories and files that all files cannot be viewed on one screen, you can connect the output of DIR to the input of the MORE command.

A filter command uses a pipe. This is the "|" symbol on your keyboard. Let's suppose that there are two filters: "filter_1" and "filter_2". The following is the command that DR DOS uses to link these filters together:

```
source | filter_1 | filter_2
```

Source is a command similar to TYPE that writes its output to the screen. This command now writes its output to a temporary file during the execution of the command. The filter_1 command reads the data from this file and writes its output to another temporary file. The filter_2 command reads the data from this second temporary file and writes the output on the screen.

DR DOS has three filters available: SORT, MORE and FIND. We'll discuss each in this chapter.

5.1   Redirecting Data

You can also use filters to redirect data. In our examples the keyboard and screen were redirected to a temporary file. The redirection of data using the "|" symbol is called piping.

You don't have to use piping in DR DOS to redirect a file. If you want to run a file through a filter, activate the filter as follows:

```
filter < input_file > output_file
```

The filter reads the data from the input file and writes it to the output file. If you leave the name of the output file off, the filter writes the output to the screen. We can also use this method to redirect the output of a filter to the printer:

```
filter < input_file > LPT1
```

For example, to create and sort a list of the files from the current directory and then print the filenames with the .TXT extension, type the following:

```
DIR | SORT | FIND ".TXT" > LPT1 [Enter]
```

If there are several files in the directory, you can save time by rearranging the SORT and FIND filters because there will be fewer lines to sort.

Automatic
Parking

To conclude this section, we'll give you an example for redirecting keyboard input. Say you have a laptop computer with a hard disk that requires you to execute an external PARK command before switching it off. (Note: PARK is not part of DR DOS and should be supplied by the manufacturer of your computer or hard disk.)

You can write a batch file called P.BAT to park the hard drive with a simple P. The following line must be in the P.BAT file:

```
PARK <Y.TST
```

The Y.TST file from which P.BAT reads data must be entered as follows:

```
Y [Enter]
```

When P.BAT is executed, the PARK command is also executed. Then the character "Y" is read from the Y.TST, rather than prompting you to enter Y from the keyboard.

Not all programs and commands accept piping from the keyboard and the screen. You should examine these individually. Be careful in creating the files that bypass keyboard input. An error could crash the system because it's waiting for the user to press the right key, which will never happen.

The devices of DR DOS can also be used as targets for piping. You can use the following devices:

Device	Example	Input	Output
CON	keyboard and screen	yes	yes
COM1	serial interface 1	yes	yes
COMn	serial interface n	yes	yes
PRN or LPT1	parallel interface 1	no	yes
LPTn	parallel interface n	no	yes
NUL	null (dummy) device	yes	yes

Here are some items of interest about the above devices:

- LPT can be programmed for input as well as output, and is used with some file transfer applications.

- Any output sent to the NUL device is lost. Consider this the garbage collector of DR DOS.

If you use commands like CHKDSK as starting points for pipes, you should check to see whether the command expects you to press a key. You won't receive any messages on the screen from this command. If input on the keyboard is necessary, execute the command once and note all of the keys that you press. Then use the Editor and enter the key presses just as you noted and save them in a file. Then use piping to assign the file to the command.

5.2   SORT

SORT redirects the standard input into ascending or descending sequence and rewrites them to the standard output file.

To see the directory of the current drive displayed in alphabetical order, type the following:

DIR|SORT (Enter)

You can use the following switches:

R	Performs reverse order alphanumeric sorting (high-low or Z-A).
N+	Starts the sort on column "n" of the line. For example, you could sort a disk directory by size by starting the sort at column 12.

You can also use SORT to redirect the standard input and standard output files using the < and > characters. If you wanted to sort a file named INPUT and rewrite the sorted data in a file named OUTPUT, type the following:

SORT <INPUT> OUTPUT (Enter)

To avoid overwriting the contents of the input file, we recommend using different names for both files.

If you wanted to sort the CONFIG.SYS file in reverse alphabetical order based on the second column, type the following:

TYPE CONFIG.SYS | SORT /R/+2 (Enter)

The original CONFIG.SYS file would appear on the screen similar to the following:

```
SHELL=C:\COMMAND.COM C:\ /P /E:512
BREAK=ON
HIBUFFERS=15
FILES=20
FCBS=4,4
FASTOPEN=512
LASTDRIVE=C
HISTORY=ON, 512, ON
COUNTRY=001,,C:\DRDOS\COUNTRY.SYS
HIDOS=ON
```

Unsorted CONFIG.SYS

The sorted CONFIG.SYS file would appear on the screen similar to the following:

```
BREAK=ON
COUNTRY=001,,C:\DRDOS\COUNTRY.SYS
HISTORY=ON, 512, ON
FILES=20
HIDOS=ON
HIBUFFERS=15
SHELL=C:\COMMAND.COM C:\ /P /E:512
DEVICE=C:\SSTORDRV.SYS
FCBS=4,4
FASTOPEN=512
LASTDRIVE=C
```

Reverse sorted CONFIG.SYS by second characters

SORT does not distinguish between uppercase or lowercase letters.

You can chain SORT to another DR DOS command using the pipe symbol to send the output of the first command to the second command. The following command sorts the directory and outputs it to the printer:

```
DIR | SORT > PRN (Enter)
```

5.3 MORE

MORE is used to prevent the screen contents from scrolling. It temporarily halts the screen output of longer files (such as a directory) before they scroll off the screen.

MORE usually is used with other DR DOS commands such as DIR and TYPE. For example, to display the contents of a large subdirectory, type the following:

```
DIR | MORE (Enter)
```

When all but the last line of the screen is filled, the following message appears:

```
Strike a key when ready . . .
```

DR DOS waits for you to strike (press) any key to continue the directory display.

The following command line creates and displays information from a special temporary file containing information provided by CHKDSK. Since all information must be saved in the temporary file first, your computer may appear to freeze before the display begins.

```
CHKDSK C:/V | MORE (Enter)
```

5.4 FIND

Use the FIND command to search for character strings in a group of text files. By adding the FIND command to the CHKDSK command, we can view all the .EXE files on a disk drive:

```
CHKDSK C:/V | FIND ".EXE" | MORE  Enter
```

This command will display all of the .EXE files on the disk similar to the following:

```
CHKDSK C:/V | FIND "EXE" | MORE




C:\DRDOS\NLSFUNC.EXE
C:\DRDOS\SHARE.EXE
C:\DRDOS\APPEND.EXE
C:\DRDOS\TASKMAX.EXE
C:\DRDOS\MEMMAX.EXE
C:\DRDOS\XCOPY.EXE
C:\DRDOS\XDEL.EXE
C:\DRDOS\XDIR.EXE
C:\DRDOS\FASTOPEN.EXE
C:\DRDOS\MEM.EXE
C:\DRDOS\UNINSTAL.EXE
C:\DRDOS\DISKOPT.EXE
C:\DRDOS\UNDELETE.EXE
C:\DRDOS\DELWATCH.EXE
C:\DRDOS\DISKMAP.EXE
C:\DRDOS\DELPURGE.EXE
C:\DRDOS\LOCK.EXE
C:\DRDOS\EDITOR.EXE
C:\DRDOS\MOVE.EXE
C:\DRDOS\LOGIN.EXE
C:\DRDOS\SUBST.EXE
C:\DRDOS\RENDIR.EXE
C:\DRDOS\SCRIPT.EXE
Strike a key when ready . . .
```

To search for a string containing quotation marks, you must enter each quote mark as a double quote (""). For example:

```
FIND /c " said, ""This is great!""," demo.txt  Enter
```

You can chain two FIND commands together to search an entire file for two specific strings. For example, to find all of the lines of a Pascal program containing a BEGIN statement and a comment, enter the following:

```
FIND "BEGIN" DEMO.PAS | FIND "C*"  Enter
```

Use the DR DOS wildcard characters (* and ?) to specify multiple files. See Section 3.7 for information on wildcards.

The following list shows the switches available for you to use with FIND.

? or H	Display help screen.
B	Changes display format of the list. This allows you to have descriptive headings.
F	Show only the names of files containing a specified string.
V	Inverts the search process so that the lines which do not contain the specified string are displayed or counted.
N	Numbers the display lines. The number is displayed in square brackets without leading zeros.
C	The number of lines containing the string are only counted and not displayed.
S	Searches for files in subdirectories of the current directory.
U	Case-sensitive search.

6. ViewMAX

6.   ViewMAX

DR DOS includes ViewMAX, a graphical user interface that lets you easily execute all DR DOS file operations. This means you do not actually need to type anything to use DR DOS. ViewMAX serves as an alternative method of communication between you and DR DOS.

The ViewMAX interface is composed of a set of commands arranged across a menu bar. When you select each option, a list of commands is displayed. We'll discuss these options and commands in Section 6.3.

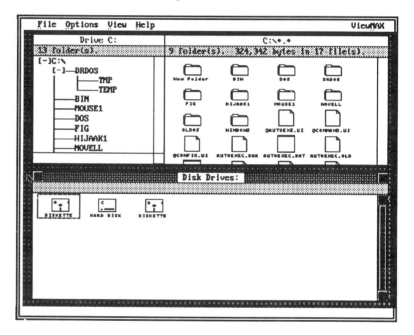

ViewMAX

6.1 Starting ViewMAX

When installing DR DOS, you can specify whether ViewMAX is to be automatically run each time the computer is started (booted). If you choose this option, the ViewMAX command is placed in the AUTOEXEC.BAT file and appears as soon as the computer starts.

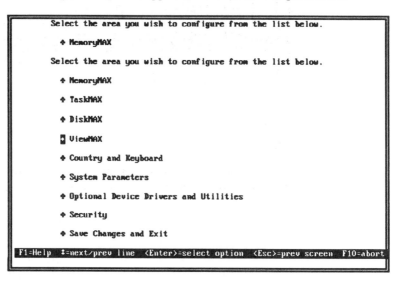

Using SETUP to install ViewMAX

You can also start ViewMAX manually by typing the ViewMAX command from the DR DOS system prompt:

VIEWMAX (Enter)

When ViewMAX is installed, you will see a display similar to the following figure:

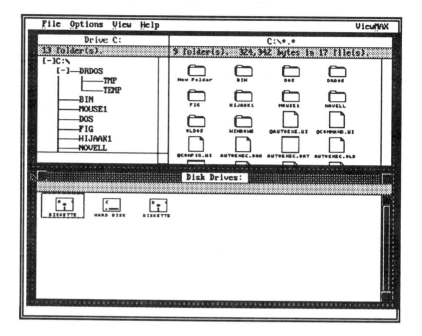

The ViewMAX main screen

Notice the narrow line which appears on the top border of the screen and displays the words *File, Options, View, Help and ViewMAX*. This is called the menu bar.

Below the menu bar are three windows. The top half of the screen is split into two windows. The left window displays the contents of the current drive in a tree structure. The right window displays the contents of the selected directory. This is referred to as *split-window mode*.

The bottom window displays the disk drives of your computer. The drives are automatically detected by ViewMAX. Any substituted or Network drives are also displayed.

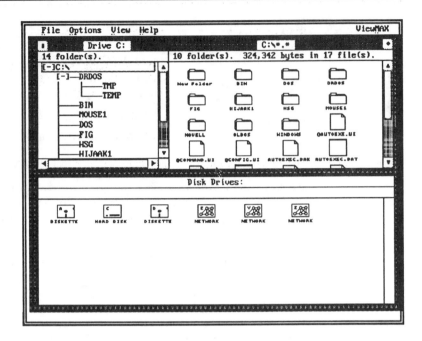

ViewMAX displaying three network drives

The windows contain information about your work or application. There are several functions which you can perform on an individual window. The arrow keys (⬆⬅➡⬇) may be used to move within a window. Pressing (Tab) switches between windows.

Using
ViewMAX

Menus are displayed and commands selected by pressing the (Alt) key in combination with other keys.

A mouse may be used with ViewMAX. Move the mouse pointer around the screen. Press the left mouse button to make your selections. ViewMAX must have been configured to use a mouse before the mouse pointer is displayed.

Terminology

A few terms must be explained before our discussion of ViewMAX can continue.

Drag	To press and hold the mouse button while moving the mouse.
Rubber rectangle	A rectangle which expands and contracts on the screen as the mouse pointer is dragged.

Shift-clicking   A technique for selecting multiple items at the
                        same time. Click on the first item, then hold
                        down the (Shift) key while pointing to and
                        clicking the mouse button on the remaining
                        items to be selected.

Deselecting   Canceling a selection. Point to an open area of
                        the window and click the mouse button.

Menu Display   The ViewMAX menus contain the commands for ViewMAX operations.

File   Options   View   Help

The menu bar shown above contains the titles of the menus. Each menu
title has one character underlined; F for the File menu, O for the Options
menu, V for the View menu, H for the Help menu and M for the
ViewMAX menu (not shown).

These menus can be opened by pressing (Alt) and the key corresponding to
the underlined character in the menu bar.

Menus may also be activated by pointing to them with the mouse pointer
and clicking the mouse button.

You can have only one window active at one time. Press the (Tab) key to
move between the windows. A highlighted title bar indicates which
window is active. You can move the mouse pointer to select between the
two windows. Move the mouse pointer to the desired symbol and activate
it by double clicking the mouse button.

While we won't address each individual command of ViewMAX, we
would like to show you how you can move around in the graphic user
interface. You can select the different options using either the keyboard or
the mouse.

6.2   Opening Files

Before executing some commands, you must tell ViewMAX the file on which to operate. DR DOS provides two methods of selecting the file.

How to Open
a File

When using the keyboard, position the selection frame on the desired file and then press either the (Spacebar) or the (Enter) key. If you're using the mouse, simply click on the file.

To open the selected file using the keyboard, press the (Alt)+(F) (O) key combination. To open a file using the mouse, double-click the file.

To close the file and return to the main ViewMAX screen, press the (Alt)+(F4) key combination.

Make certain to have a diskette in a floppy disk drive before opening that drive. You may lock up or crash the system if no diskette is present in the selected disk drive.

6.3   Menus and Commands

ViewMAX
Menus

The menu structure of ViewMAX is quite versatile. Many functions can be controlled from the menu. The information presented here is only intended to provide a brief summation of each menu function. Refer to your DR DOS 6.0 ViewMAX User Guide for complete information.

Let's look at the menu bar — File, Options, View, Help and ViewMAX.

Notice that one letter in each option is underlined. If you want to open, or display, any of the menus, press (Alt) and the underlined letter of the desired menu. When using a mouse, point to the menu title and click on it.

For example, to display the commands of the File menu, you must press the (Alt) and (F) keys at the same time. You can now use the arrow keys to move the selection bar through the menu, or to an adjacent menu title.

Using a Mouse

If you're using a mouse, move the mouse pointer to the desired command and click the left mouse button. You can also use the arrow keys to move within the menu commands. Choose a command by clicking the left mouse key or pressing the (Enter) key. You can also type the underlined letter within that menu command.

Some commands will appear ghosted or not displayed in bold letters. This means that you cannot select this particular command at that time. You'll also see that the selection frame cannot be positioned on this command.

Press (Esc) to close any open menu.

File menu

This menu contains the commands that you'll use to control file management including copying, deleting, renaming and returning to DR DOS.

Keyboard:	Press (Alt)+(F).
Mouse:	Move the mouse pointer to the ViewMAX menu bar and then to the word File. Press the left mouse button.

The following menu commands are displayed when you select the File menu:

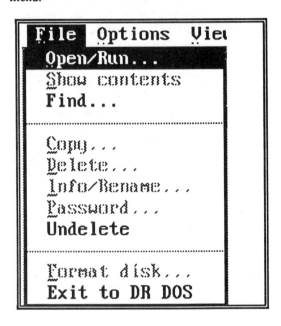

File menu

The following table shows the ViewMAX commands in the File menu and provides a brief explanation of the command. Again, notice that one letter in each command is underlined. If you want to access the command, press (Alt) and the underlined letter.

ViewMAX	DR DOS Commands
Open/Run...	Opens the currently selected file or folder, or runs an application.
Show contents	Displays the contents of the selected file as readable text or in hexadecimal form.
Find	Finds the specified file, then displays it as a highlighted icon in the active window.
Copy...	Allows the selected files or folders to be copied to another window.
Delete...	Deletes all selected items. Undelete can be used to recover the files.
Info/Rename...	Displays information about the currently selected item and permits renaming it.
Password...	Used to assign passwords for controlling access to files.
Format disk...	Formats your currently selected diskette.
Exit to DR DOS	Quits ViewMAX and returns to the command line of the DR DOS operating system.

Options menu

This menu contains the commands specific to ViewMAX. These commands affect mouse control and the confirmation of deletes, copies and overwrites.

Keyboard:	Press (Alt)+(O).
Mouse:	Move the mouse pointer to the ViewMAX menu bar and then to the word Options. Press the left mouse button.

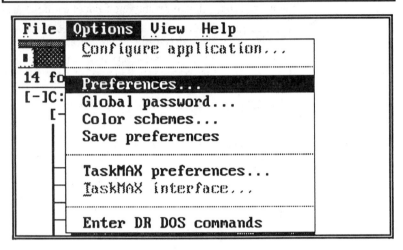

Options menu

The following table shows the ViewMAX commands in the Options menu and provides a brief explanation of the command:

ViewMAX Options Menu	Explanation
Configure Application	Specifies how you want an application to work in ViewMAX.
Preferences	Permits specifying some aspects of how ViewMAX works.
Global password...	Specifies a password to be used whenever a folder or document is password protected.
Color Schemes	Permits selecting the color schemes used in ViewMAX.
Save preferences...	Saves current preferences and Window arrangement.
TaskMAX Preferences	Permits specifying how TaskMAX operates from ViewMAX.
TaskMAX Interface	Permits switching to other applications from ViewMAX.
Enter DR DOS commands	Allows you to enter DR DOS commands without leaving ViewMAX.

View menu

This menu controls the appearance of the folders and files on the screen.
For example, you can display the folders by icons, text, type, size or date.

Keyboard:	Press Alt+V.
Mouse:	Move the mouse pointer to the ViewMAX menu bar and then to the word View. Press the left mouse button.

The following pictures should appear on your screen when you select the
File menu:

The ViewMAX View menu

The following table shows the ViewMAX command in the View menu
and a brief explanation of the command:

ViewMAX	DR DOS Commands
Close [Alt]+[F4]	Closes the current folder and redisplays the previous folder or directory.
Resize [Alt]+[F5]	Switches the display size of the current window between full or half screen.
Refresh [F5]	Refreshes the active window to display its current contents.
Show tree	Displays the folders as a tree structure in one window and the contents of a selected folder in another window.
Show as text	Displays the current windows folders and files as text instead of icons.
Show as icons	Displays the current windows folders and files as icons instead of text.
Name order	SORT (by name)
Type order	SORT (by type)
Size order	SORT (by size)
Date order	SORT (by date)
Wildcards	Allows you to display a subset of the files by using the wildcard characters * and ?.

Help menu

Select this menu when you need information on windows, menus or a dialog.

Keyboard:	Press [Alt]+[H].
Mouse:	Move the mouse pointer to the ViewMAX menu bar and then to the word Help. Press the left mouse button.

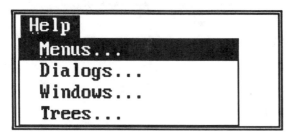

Help menu

The following table shows the ViewMAX commands in the Help menu and explanation of the command:

ViewMAX	DR DOS Commands
Menus	Displays summary Help screen for menus.
Dialogs...	Displays summary Help screen for dialogs.
Windows...	Displays summary Help screen for windows.
Trees	Displays a help screen for the left window in split-window mode.

ViewMAX menu

The ViewMAX menu displays information on the current release of ViewMAX. It also provides a calculator and clock desk accessories.

Keyboard:	Press Alt+M.
Mouse:	Move the mouse pointer to the ViewMAX menu bar and then to the word ViewMAX. Press the left mouse button.

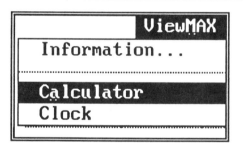

ViewMAX menu

The following picture shows the ViewMAX calculator:

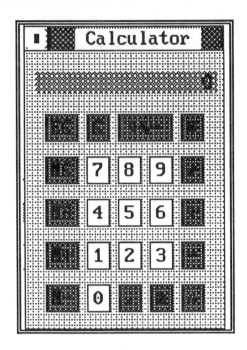

ViewMAX calculator

Calculator   The DR DOS calculator works exactly like a pocket or desktop calculator.

You can access calculator functions from your keyboard:

E+C	Clears the current entry
Enter	Same as the equal sign on the calculator
C	Ends current calculation
Num Lock	Allows you to use the numeric keypad
Tab	Closes the calculator window

The DR DOS calculator has a memory function:

Ⓜ+⊕	Adds the figure to memory
Ⓜ+⊖	Deletes the figure from memory
Ⓜ+Ⓡ	Recalls present value from memory
Ⓜ+Ⓒ	Clears value from memory

Clock

The clock desk accessory displays the current time and date. Use the arrow keys and number keys to reset the time or date. You must reset each value individually.

To set the alarm, press the (Enter) key to switch the clock from date mode to alarm mode. This resets the time display to 12.00 AM (also notice the uppercase A in front of the time display).

Use the ⊕ and ⊕ arrow keys to highlight the hour, minute and am/pm for the alarm to sound. Then press the number key corresponding to the hour you want the alarm to sound. Then repeat this step for the minute. Press the ⊕ arrow key to toggle between am/pm.

Press the (Spacebar) key to activate the alarm. The small musical note is highlighted when you activate the alarm.

Press (Alt)+(F4) to close the clock window.

6.4 Dialogs

You may have wondered what the three dots (...) indicate following several of the ViewMAX commands. These dots indicate that a dialog will appear whenever you select these commands.

DR DOS displays a dialog when you need to read additional information or type additional information for ViewMAX.

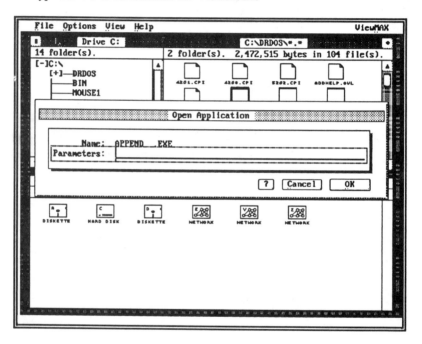

You can move between the fields or options of a dialog by pressing the (Tab) key or arrow keys. When the appropriate option or button is selected, press the (Enter) key.

A button is an option surrounded by a rectangular border. You have three methods available to select a specific button.

1. Move the mouse pointer onto it and press the left mouse button.

2. Use the arrow keys or ⌐Tab⌐ key to move the selection frame to the desired button. Then press either the ⌐Spacebar⌐ or ⌐Enter⌐ key.

3. Use the key combination of ⌐Alt⌐ and the underlined letter of the desired button.

You can exit the dialog by pressing the ⌐Esc⌐ key.

What is a Folder?

After opening the desired folder, all files are displayed as icons. Notice that the selection frame is surrounding the icon called "New Folder". A folder is the equivalent of a DR DOS directory or subdirectory.

Press ⌐Enter⌐ to open the new folder or use the arrow keys to select another icon (file). You can supply a name for the new folder when you try to open it.

Copying Files

The ViewMAX Copy... command copies files from one window to another window. Therefore, one window shows the icon you're copying and the other window must show the destination for the copy. If you want to copy from one window to another window.

If you want to copy a file onto the diskette in drive A:, press ⌐Tab⌐ to open the window corresponding to drive A:. If you want to copy into a folder (directory), select that folder and press the ⌐Enter⌐ key.

Then press ⌐Tab⌐ to move to the second window. Use the arrow keys to select the file you want to copy. When the desired file is selected, press ⌐Alt⌐+⌐F⌐ ⌐C⌐ to open the Copy... command.

This opens a new dialog. Press ⌐Enter⌐ to accept the command or ⌐Tab⌐+⌐Enter⌐ to cancel the Copy... command. The file you copied will appear next to the folder.

Renaming Files

Press ⌐Tab⌐ (if necessary) to activate the window displaying the file you want to rename. Use the arrow keys to select the desired file so that the gray selection frame surrounds the icon. Press the ⌐Spacebar⌐ to select it.

The Info/Rename... command is in the File menu, so press ⌐Alt⌐+⌐F⌐ ⌐I⌐ to open the Info/Rename... command. This opens the following screen:

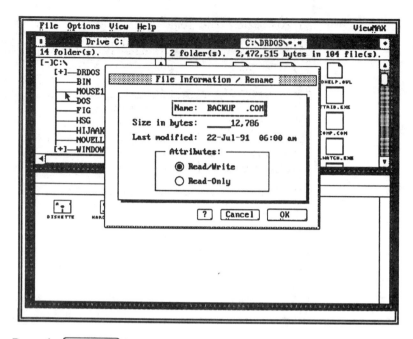

Press the (Backspace) key to erase the old filename. Then type in the new filename (remember not to exceed 8 characters). When you're satisfied that the new filename is correct, press (Alt)+(O) to select the OK button.

Deleting Files   To delete a file, use the arrow keys to move the rectangular selection frame to the desired file. Press the (Spacebar) to select the file. Then press the (Alt)+(F) (D) key combination for the ViewMAX Delete... command. The following dialog appears:

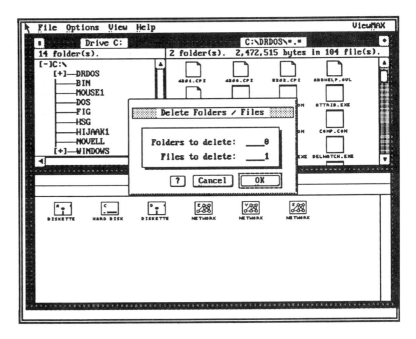

To delete the selected file, press [Alt]+[O]. Press [Esc] to exit the dialog
without deleting the file.

7. TaskMAX

7. TaskMAX

As you work with your computer, you'll often find it necessary to switch between applications to perform your work. This process can become laborious as you save a file and close one application, open another application, then load a necessary data file, then close that application to move to a third.

DR DOS 6.0 addresses and simplifies these chores by providing *TaskMAX*, a fast, efficient utility for switching between tasks. TaskMAX uses extended or expanded memory for storing tasks. This means that switching between tasks is almost instantaneous.

When all available memory is used, files are automatically swapped to your hard disk. This means that TaskMAX can handle up to 20 different applications easily and efficiently. Instead of using your valuable low memory area, which is needed by your applications, TaskMAX will be automatically installed into the High Memory Area (HMA) (the area above 640K), if sufficient memory is available.

Applications you use frequently can be loaded and instantly available every time you turn on your computer. You can even run several copies of the same application. Even more important, it's easy to copy information between applications.

Installing
TaskMAX

The easiest way to configure and install TaskMAX is to use the DR DOS SETUP program.

From the system prompt, type:

SETUP (Enter)

Then continue to press (Enter) until the configuration screen appears, as shown in the following figure.

107

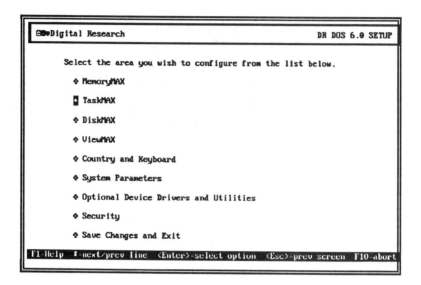

Configuring TaskMAX from SETUP

Select the TaskMAX option, then press (Enter).

The following screen will appear:

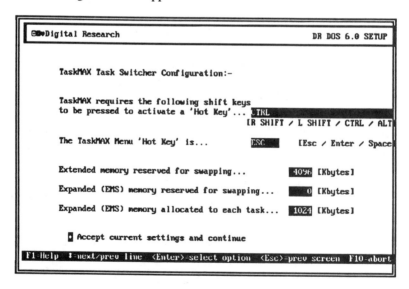

TaskMAX switcher configuration

This screen permits selecting the "Hot Keys", the TaskMAX menu activation key, and defining how TaskMAX should use memory.

The first field permits specifying the Shift keys which must be pressed in conjunction with another key to activate a TaskMAX "Hot Key". For example, if you select Ctrl, Alt and Enter as the "Hot Keys", these keys must be pressed to activate the TaskMAX menu.

Next select the "Hot Key" for activating the TaskMAX menu.

The default settings are Ctrl + Esc, but can be changed by pressing the right and left cursor keys (← and →) to cycle through the available options. Select your "Hot Keys" so as not to conflict with keys used for other functions by your applications programs.

The extended memory field permits specifying the amount of extended memory (the area of memory above 1Mb) that will be reserved for task switching. Using this area of memory will reduce the amount for task switching, but will also reduce the amount of extended memory available for use by your applications.

Once the extended memory area is exhausted, TaskMAX will swap background task to your hard disk.

Expanded Memory   The Expanded (EMS) field permits specifying an amount of expanded memory to be reserved for task swapping. This is handy on computers without Extended memory.

Finally, you can prevent a single application from reserving all available EMS (expanded memory) by specifying the amount of memory which will be seen by the application. This will permit more than one application to utilize expanded memory at the same time.

After you are satisfied with your configuration settings, move the cursor to the bottom of the screen and accept the configuration options by pressing Enter.

Next, the configuration program will ask whether TaskMAX should be loaded when DR DOS boots, and you can also specify the directory for storing tasks swapped to your hard disk when memory is full.

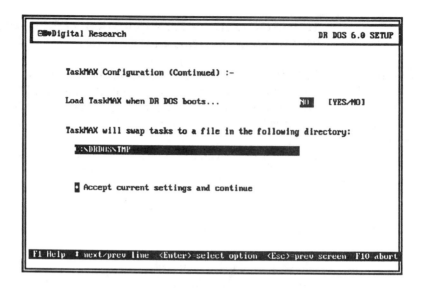

Setting TaskMAX for autobooting

TaskMAX has now been configured. Continue to press ⟨Enter⟩ to return to the Configuration Screen, then select the final option, "Save changes and Exit" and press ⟨Enter⟩.

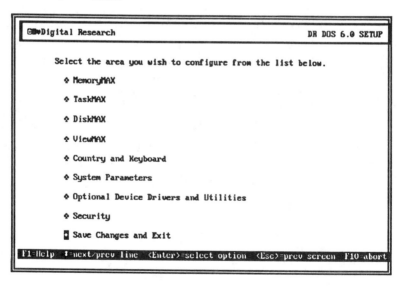

Save and exit

The TASKMAX.INI file will be updated and your changes will take affect when your computer is rebooted.

Running
TaskMAX
from the
command line

TaskMAX can be configured from the command line, but you cannot change the default keys. If you originally configured TaskMAX from SETUP, any changes made from the command line are only in affect for the current session.

The syntax for installing TaskMAX from the command line is:

```
TASKMAX [/?|H] [D=dirpath] [/X[=nnnn]] [/E[=nnnn]]
[/L=nnnn]] [/C command] [/N[:nn][name]]
```

Command
Switches

The following chart offers a brief explanation of the TaskMAX switches.

Switch	Meaning
/? or /H	Displays help screen.
/D=*dirpath*	Directory to be used for swapping background tasks to the hard disk.
/X[=*nnnn*]	Size of the memory area reserved for swapping background tasks. If no parameters are entered with the /X switch, all available memory is used.
/E[=*nnnn*]	Swaps tasks to extended memory. *nnnn* is the amount of memory reserved. If no value is entered for *nnnn*, all available memory is used.
/L=*nnnn*	Sets a limit on the amount of expanded memory used for each task.
/C *command*	Permits adding a task to the TaskMAX menu, where *command* is the name of the task to be added.

When DR DOS automatically installs TaskMAX upon booting, a message will be displayed informing you of this, and reminding you which keys can be used for task switching.

7.1 Using TaskMAX

Warning!　　Any TSR (terminate and stay resident) programs that you use must be loaded before TaskMAX. Modify your AUTOEXEC.BAT file appropriately.

TaskMAX is very easy to use. Either install it from the command line, or use SETUP as explained in the previous section to install automatically when your computer is booted. A message similar to the following will be displayed when TaskMAX is automatically loaded:

```
TaskMAX R1.00   Application Switcher
Copyright (c) 1989,1991 Digital Research Inc. All rights reserved.

The DR DOS application switcher is now loaded.
Use Ctrl+Esc to display the TaskMAX menu,
 or Ctrl+number to switch between existing tasks.
```

TaskMAX autoboot screen

Display the TaskMAX menu by pressing Ctrl+Esc. The TaskMAX menu will be displayed at the top of the screen. The menu is divided into two parts; the left side contains the task list, while the right side shows the TaskMAX options.

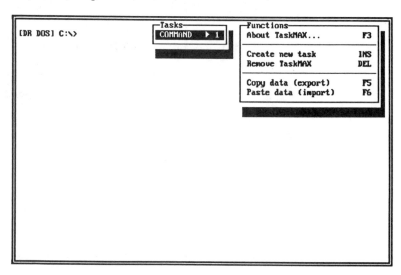

TaskMAX menu

The TaskMAX menu has five options: *About TaskMAX..., Create new task, Remove TaskMax, Copy data (export), Paste data (import)*.

About TaskMAX

Selecting *About TaskMAX* by pressing (F3) displays a dialog containing information about TaskMAX's status. Valuable information about the amount of free swap space and the percentage of remaining free space can be found here.

Press (Esc) to return to the TaskMAX menu.

Adding Tasks

To add a task, first display the TaskMAX menu by pressing (Ctrl)+(Esc), then select *Create new task* by pressing (Ins). You will be returned to the DR DOS command line.

Start the application you want added. Press (Ctrl)+(Esc) to display the TaskMAX menu and you will see that the application you have just loaded is shown in the left menu as task 2. Subsequently loaded tasks will be shown with numbers assigned to them. Repeat this process to add more applications to the task list. TaskMAX can control up to 20 tasks.

You can switch between tasks by calling the menu and pressing the corresponding number, or by pressing (Ctrl) plus the task number assigned when the application was loaded.

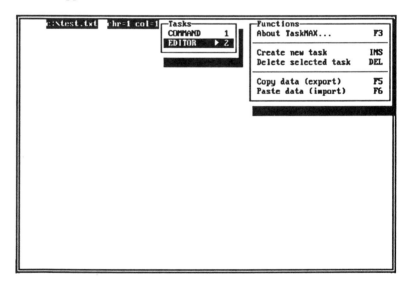

EDITOR installed as task 2

113

Deleting Tasks To remove a task from the list, use the cursor keys to position the highlighted area over the name of the task to be removed and press ⌈Del⌋. You will switch to that task and a dialog will ask if the task should be deleted. Press ⌈Y⌋ to delete the task, or ⌈N⌋ to cancel the deletion and return to the TaskMAX menu.

Removing TaskMAX may be removed from memory by closing all tasks, then
TaskMAX pressing ⌈Del⌋ from the TaskMAX menu.

Copying Data Data may be copied easily between applications.

Switch to the application containing the data to be copied. Display the data on the screen. Display the TaskMAX menu by pressing ⌈Ctrl⌋+⌈Esc⌋. Select Copy data (export) by pressing ⌈F5⌋.

The menu is replaced by a box displaying the keys to use when marking the rectangle to be copied. Press ⌈Enter⌋ to continue. You may press ⌈Esc⌋ to exit.

Position the top left corner of the box first by using the ⌈↓⌋ and ⌈→⌋ keys to move the highlighted area. When you have positioned this corner, press ⌈End⌋.

Now position the bottom right corner with the ⌈←⌋ and ⌈↑⌋ keys. It becomes necessary to reposition the top left corner, press the ⌈Home⌋ key and use the arrow keys to select the new position.

Pressing the ⌈Spacebar⌋ switches corners.

To cancel marking a block of text, press ⌈Esc⌋.

Pasting Data Display the TaskMAX menu and press ⌈F6⌋ to select Paste data (import).

The TaskMAX menu is replaced by a menu containing the three paste options: ASCII mode, Text mode, and Numeric mode. The paste format determines the characters at the end of every typed line. ASCII mode will work with most applications. Text and Numeric mode are generally only useful for use with spreadsheets.

For more precise and detailed information about using TaskMAX, refer to your DR DOS 6.0 User Manual.

8. DiskMAX

8. DiskMAX

The space necessary for storing applications on your hard disk is growing rapidly. This increase in storage size demands peak performance from your hard disk. DR DOS 6.0 provides several utilities for maintaining hard disk performance, such as disk optimization, a disk cache, and disk compression. These types of programs are usually only available from third-party vendors at an additional expense. Digital Research has provided an extensive set of tools as part of DR DOS 6.0.

This section provides a brief introduction to using these powerful utilities. Refer to your DR DOS 6.0 User Manual for more detailed information.

*Installing
DiskMAX*

As with most utilities options available with DR DOS 6.0, it's easiest to install the necessary programs with the SETUP program. Run SETUP and select the DiskMAX option.

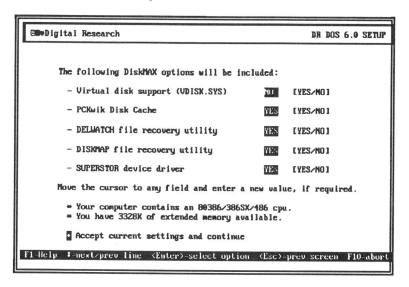

Selecting DiskMAX options from SETUP

8.1   VDISK.SYS

VDISK.SYS permits reserving a portion of your computer's memory to act as if it were a fast disk drive. The device generated by VDISK.SYS is often called a virtual disk, memory disk or RAM disk.

A virtual disk has one big advantage over a floppy diskette or hard disk: Extremely fast access. Memory requires very little access time, and loading and saving applications and data can be almost instantaneous with a virtual disk. Like anything stored in RAM, however, the information stored in a virtual disk disappears when the computer is switched off.

If you want to install a virtual disk, which can be handy for temporary disk storage use with TaskMAX, be sure to copy any data saved to the virtual disk to a floppy diskette or hard disk before switching off your computer.

When you select the Virtual Disk Support option from the DiskMAX options, DR DOS prompts you for some specifics about the size of the virtual disk in kilobytes, sector size, number of root directory entries and whether to use expanded or extended memory. Select the defaults and press Enter. After saving changes and rebooting your computer, DR DOS will include a virtual disk, which you can access as you would any normal disk. You can use it for copying files or for temporarily storing files.

To prevent problems, DR DOS prevents the user from accessing the virtual disk using the DISKCOPY or FORMAT command. Entering either command results in an error message when directed to the virtual disk.

8.2   Super PC-Kwik Disk Cache

A disk cache stores data recently accessed from your hard disk in an area of random access memory (RAM). This can increase the apparent speed of your hard disk by reducing the number of times an application must access the drive. Instead of taking frequently used data from disk, disk intensive applications can get this data from the RAM allocated by the disk cache, thus cutting disk access time.

Super PC-Kwik Disk Cache decreases the amount of time it takes your system to read information from diskettes and hard disks. It's designed to make the most efficient use of whatever type of memory is available in your computer. Super PC-Kwik Cache is a memory resident program and must be loaded into memory before it can be used. It's easiest to configure your installation of DR DOS to automatically install the cache upon booting by using the SETUP program.

Options in
SETUP

If you select the PCKwik option in SETUP, you will be prompted for information about Microsoft Windows, whether you want the cache in extended or expanded memory, automatic memory allocation and memory reserved for other applications. Once you select these options, save changes and reboot to activate Super PC-Kwik Cache.

If it becomes necessary to remove Super PC-Kwik Cache from memory, type the following at the system prompt:

SUPERPCK /U (Enter)

Microsoft
Windows Users

If you use Microsoft Windows, always load Super PC-Kwik Cache before loading Windows. If you are using Windows 3.0 in Enhanced or Standard modes on a 386 computer, use the following command to load Super PC-Kwik:

SUPERPCK /E (Enter)

then start Windows by typing:

WIN/3 (Enter)

or in standard mode by typing:

WIN/S (Enter)

Super PC-
Kwik Options

Few options are necessary for running Super PC-Kwik Cache. Here is a table listing the options available when Super PC-Kwik Cache is loaded.

Option	Meaning
/-*drive*	Do not cache *drive*. This option permits specifying which drives should be cached.
/&U-	Do not automatically move the parts of the cache that are normally in conventional memory to upper memory. The default is to load into the upper memory blocks whenever possible.
/A+	Use expanded memory for the disk cache.
/EM+	Use extended memory for the disk cache.
/L:*nnnn*	Enable the feature of Super PC-Kwik Cache that permits lending areas of memory to applications. Up to *nnnn* bytes is available for lending.
/L-	Disable lending of memory.
/P+	Display all options in effect at startup.
/R:*nnnn*	Reserve *nnnn* kilobytes after loading Super PC-Kwik Cache.
/?	Display a help screen with a summary of these options.

Some options are available for use after Super PC-Kwik Cache has been loaded and is running. Here is a table of those options with a brief description.

Options	Meaning
/D	Disable the cache, but leave in memory.
/E	Enable a previously disabled cache.
/F	Clear all data from cache.
/M	Display cache measurements.
/P	Display all options in effect.
/U	Unload Super PC-Kwik Cache.
/?	Display a summary of options.

Other options, beyond the scope of this book are also available. Refer to your DR DOS 6.0 User Manual for a complete description.

8.3 DELWATCH

DELWATCH is a special TSR (terminate and stay resident) utility program used to save files which are deleted. Any files deleted after you run DELWATCH are marked as *pending delete files* and removed from the directory structure. The file still exists on disk, and can be recovered using the UNDELETE command.

A limit for the number of files to save pending delete can be set to prevent the disk from filling with files pending deletion. When this limit is reached, DELWATCH allocates space for newer files by removing the oldest files first. To completely remove the files from the disk, use the DELPURGE command (more on this later).

A number of switches are available when installing DELWATCH from the command line, but the simplest installation method is to install it automatically with the SETUP program. DELWATCH uses the following command line switches:

Switches	Meaning
/? or /H	Display help screen.
/S	Display status of DELWATCH.
/D	Disable DELWATCH on specified drives.
/B:*nnnn*	Specifies number of files with the same name and path to save.
/O:*ext*[+*ext*...]	Saves only files with specified extensions.
/E:*ext*[+*ext*...]	Saves all files except with specified extensions.
/M:*nnn*	Specifies the maximum number of files to save. The default limit is 200.

DELPURGE   DELPURGE frees the disk space occupied by files marked as pending delete by DELWATCH. DELPURGE uses the following command switches:

121

Switches	Meaning
/?: or /H	Display help screen.
/A	Remove specified files without prompt.
/L	List specified files, but do not delete them.
/S	Remove files in subdirectories lower than the specified subdirectory.
/P	Pause before removing specified files.
/D:*date*	Remove files deleted before the specified date, or files deleted before the last *nn* days.
/T:*time*	Remove file deleted before the specified time only.

8.4   DISKMAP

The DISKMAP utility provides a means of saving information about deleted files which is used by UNDELETE during file recovery operations.

The FAT (File Allocation Table) is an index located on every disk which is used by the operating system to locate files. DISKMAP makes a copy of the current File Allocation Table (FAT) on a disk. This copy is replaced every time DISKMAP is run. The DISKMAP command is automatically placed in your AUTOEXEC.BAT file when DR DOS 6.0 is installed, and executes every time your computer is booted.

DISKMAP provides a pointer to the original location of a deleted file. If the space has not been used by another file, UNDELETE can use this information to recover the file.

One advantage of using DISKMAP instead of DELWATCH is that DISKMAP does not use any of your application memory. DISKMAP's primary disadvantage lies in the fact that it is less reliable for recovering files than DELWATCH.

DISKMAP may be installed in your AUTOEXEC.BAT file, or you may use SETUP to configure your system to execute DISKMAP every time you return to the system prompt by using the PROMPT and SET commands.

The following command lines will define a prompt which displays "WAIT", and executes DISKMAP before displaying the current path as your system prompt, whenever you return to the system prompt. For more information refer to PROMPT in your DR DOS 6.0 User Manual.

```
SET PEXEC=C:\DRDOS\DISKMAP C:[Enter]
PROMPT $PWait....$X$H$H$H$H$H$H$H$H$H$H$P$G[Enter]
```

DISKMAP uses the following command line switches:

Switch	Meaning
/? or /H	Display help screen.
/D	Erase any existing DISKMAP file.

8.5 DISKOPT

DISKOPT optimizes the performance of your hard disk. Other versions of DOS don't include utility programs such as this, although they are available from third-party manufacturers.

The DISKOPT program is menu driven and moves data on the disk to make files contiguous, relocate all free space to the end of the disk, and even sort directories. The only parameter to be specified is the designation of the drive to be optimized. For example, typing the following at the command line instructs DISKOPT to optimize drive C:

DISKOPT C: Enter

To display a help screen, type:

DISKOPT /? Enter

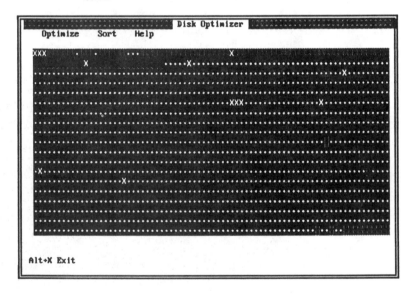

The DISKOPT screen

DISKOPT has three menus: The Optimize menu, the Sort menu and the Help menu.

Optimize   The Optimize menu has three commands. You can change to another disk for optimization, start the optimization process or exit DISKOPT.

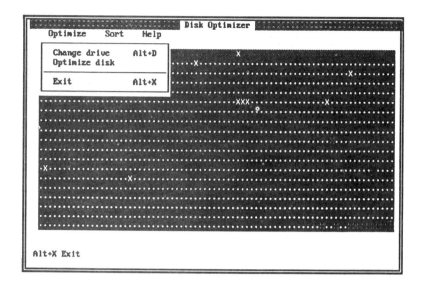

The DISKOPT Optimize menu

Sort   The Sort menu lets you specify the disk sort criteria, based on filenames, extensions, dates, file sizes, cluster, or optimization without sorting.

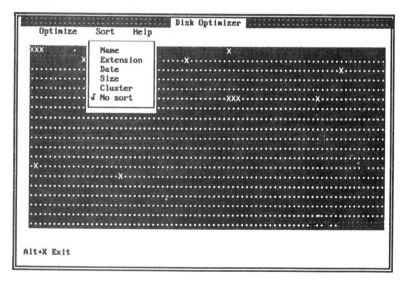

The DISKOPT Sort menu

Help   The Help menu offers online help for DISKOPT.

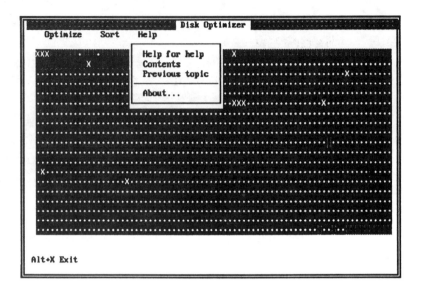

The DISKOPT Help menu

8.6   SuperStor

Regardless of the size of your disk drive, you'll eventually reach a point where the storage capacity of your drive is insufficient. It seems your need to store information will always exceed the amount of space on your drive.

Usually the solution is to remove all outdated files, delete applications that aren't absolutely necessary, and transfer as much information as possible to floppy diskettes.

This is still the best solution, but DR DOS offers a way to compress data for more efficient storage on your disk with SuperStor. SuperStor can dramatically increase the storage capacity of your hard disk. Depending on the type of files, you can more than double the drive capacity.

Best of all, SuperStor is easy to use. Once it's installed and running, no additional steps are required. Compressed drives are used as you would use any drive. Data is automatically compressed and decompressed as you read from and write to the drive.

Up to eight SuperStor partitions can be created on your system. The maximum size for a SuperStor partition is 512Mb.

Typical compression ratios are shown in the following table:

Type of Data	Compression Ration
.EXE (program) files	1.4:1 to 2:1
Word processing files	2:1 to 4:1
Database files	2:1 to 4:1
Spreadsheet files	2:1 to 4:1
Video Image files	2:1 to 8:1
CAD/CAM	3:1 to 8:1

SuperStor can also save disk space because space is reserved in sector units (usually 512 bytes) while a standard DOS disk reserves space in 2048 to 4096 byte units.

Getting ready for SuperStor

Although SuperStor is very easy to use, a few steps of preparation are necessary before compressing your disk.

1. Data is converted during the compression process. Although this process is generally safe, a disk or power failure could cause loss of all data on your disk. Make a backup copy of your hard disk either with the DR DOS BACKUP command or one of the other backup utility programs available.

2. If any copy protected software is installed on your drive, remove it. It will be necessary to reinstall copy protected software after your drive has been prepared for SuperStor.

3. Remove any Windows permanent swap files.

4. Run CHKDSK to make sure your system doesn't contain any errors.

5. Exit any multitasking environment (e.g., Windows) before running SuperStor.

6. Make sure your drive has at least 1Mb of free space. Use the DIR command to confirm that enough space exists.

Warning!!

Once SuperStor is installed on a drive, it cannot be uninstalled. Make sure all important data has been backed up and that you really want to use SuperStor before continuing.

Installing SuperStor

Although SuperStor is a complex program, there really isn't much that you need to understand to use it. This section is intended to assist you in installing SuperStor to optimize your drive storage capacity.

SSTORDRV.SYS must be loaded before you can use SSTOR.EXE, the SuperStor program. This driver can best be installed with SETUP by selecting to install the SuperStor device driver from the DiskMAX Options menu.

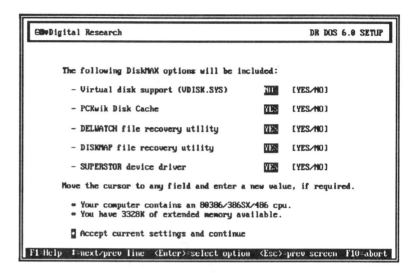

DiskMAX Options menu with SuperStor Device Driver selected

SuperStor can compress an entire disk, or it can also leave a specific amount of the disk uncompressed.

To run the SuperStor program, terminate all applications, including TaskMAX, and return to the system prompt. Type the following line:

SSTOR (Enter)

As the program begins, you will see a screen as shown below:

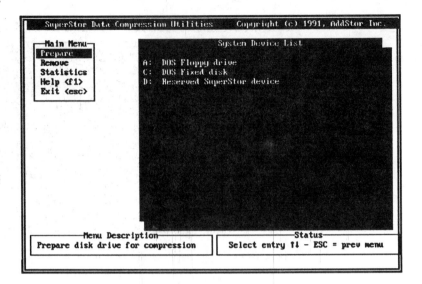

The initial SuperStor Screen

Several options are available and are explained briefly below.

Option	Function
Prepare	Formats and initializes a compressed fixed partition.
Statistics	Displays information about SuperStor drives.
Help	Displays online help about a selected item.
Exit	Return to the DR DOS system prompt.

Do the following to prepare for SuperStor:

1.   Select the *Prepare* option from the SuperStor menu. If more than one drive exists, you will be asked to specify the drive to install as a SuperStor drive.

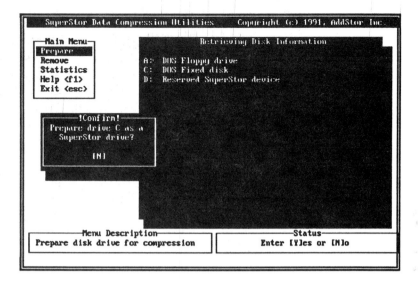

Preparing the C: drive for compression

2. After confirming your selection and pressing ⌈Enter⌋, you will be asked how much space to reserve on the uncompressed drive. This space will be accessed by a different drive designation.

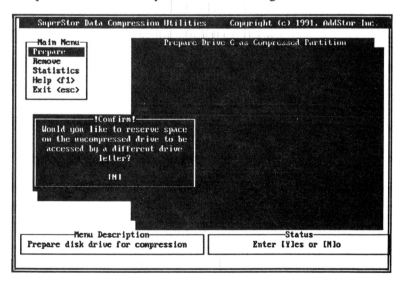

Reserving space on the uncompressed drive

If you have files such as a Windows Swap file that need to remain uncompressed, reserve enough space for those files. If you do not have any such files, compress the entire disk by selecting ⟨N⟩ and pressing ⟨Enter⟩.

3. SuperStor converts all the files on the selected drive. The time required for the compression will vary depending on the number of files stored on the drive.

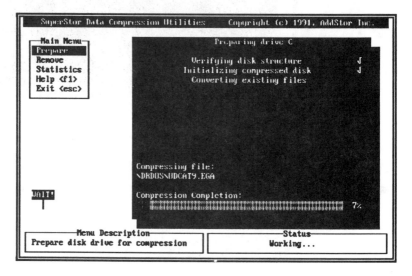

SuperStor reporting progress during drive conversion

Warning: This process cannot be aborted. Do not turn off or reset your computer. Attempting to do so can cause loss of data.

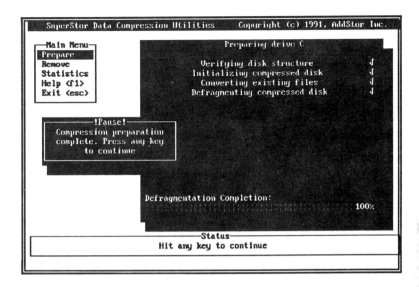

SuperStor will inform you when preparation is complete

4. When preparation is complete, select Exit to end the program. The menu offers two choices:

   RESTART which will reboot your computer. Rebooting is necessary for DR DOS to recognize a drive which has been compressed.

   EXIT which returns to the DR DOS command prompt. The newly compressed drive will not be recognized.

133

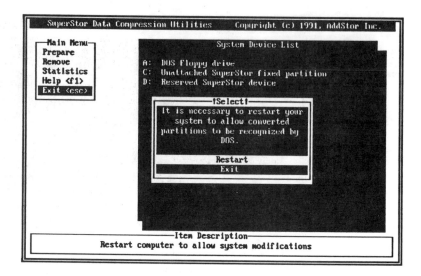

The SuperStor Exit menu

Reboot your computer so DR DOS recognizes your newly compressed drive.

Using SuperStor

The SSTOR.EXE has other uses besides preparing a drive for compression. It also provides statistics on the drive.

From the command line, type:

SSTOR (Enter)

If you have more than one compressed drive, you will be prompted to select a drive.

Select *Statistics* and a screen similar to the following figure will be displayed.

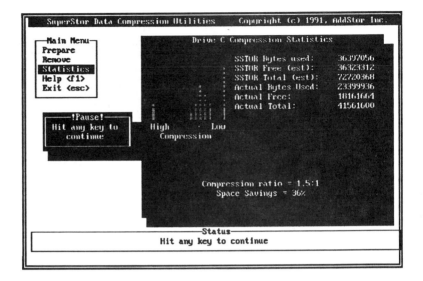

Statistical information

The following table provides a brief summary of the various entries in the Statistics Window:

Statistic	Description
SSTOR Bytes Used	This number represents the total number of bytes allocated by DR DOS for storing data on the compressed drive.
SSTOR Free (est)	This is the estimated number of bytes of data which can be stored on the compressed drive. This assumes the new data has the same compression ration as the data already on the drive.
SSTOR Total (est)	This is the total number of bytes that SuperStor estimates can be stored on the compressed drive. This number is generally greater than the physical size of the drive.
Actual Total	The physical size of the disk partition.
Actual Bytes Used	The number of bytes used by the driver to store files on the physical partition.
Actual Free	The number of bytes remaining for storing data on the physical drive.
Compression Ratio	This figure shows the efficiency of the SuperStor compression algorithm in storing data. If the compression ration is less than 1.5:1, as in the previous figure, the data is not very compressible. Consider placing this data in an uncompressed partition.
Space Savings	This is another way of expressing the compression ratio.

Select Exit or press (Esc) to exit SSTOR and return to DR DOS.

9. Memory Management

9. Memory Management

Regardless of the type, size or cost of a computer, it requires memory to operate. Your PC uses different types of memory.

Random Access Memory

Random Access Memory, or RAM, refers to the memory area where you enter information (write) and access this information (read). This information can then be erased and used again for other application programs.

RAM

RAM is the working memory or the main memory of the computer. This memory is "short term" because data is stored only as long as the computer is switched on. Therefore, the data sent to this memory is only temporarily stored in RAM. You must permanently save the data on a diskette or hard drive or lose the data after you switch off the computer.

DR DOS reserves a part of RAM for loading other applications or programs into the main memory every time you switch on the computer. These could include programs that you constantly need for working with the computer or for a certain application. For example, you may need to use an international keyboard for word processing and require special characters such as the German umlauts (ä, ö, ü).

Applications Use RAM

The largest part of RAM is used by application programs which require large amounts of memory. When you load a program exceeding the memory limits of your system, your computer displays a message indicating there is insufficient memory available. Now you have only two options: either use a program requiring less memory or increase the main memory of your computer.

Read-Only Memory

Read-Only Memory, or ROM, stores program routines that the processor requires when it starts the computer. There are two main differences between RAM and ROM:

1. Ordinarily you can only read the information in ROM (this is why it's called read-only memory).

2. The information in ROM is not lost after you switch off the computer. The system requires the information stored in ROM to run the computer.

Some manufacturers place certain programs and even applications software into ROM. The advantage of having software in ROM is that it's immediately available after booting the system. Some older IBM PCs had the BASIC programming language in ROM because at the time BASIC was considered to be *the* operating system.

A PC must have BIOS

An essential component of ROM is the Basic Input/Output System (BIOS). BIOS is a program that governs the interplay of the individual hardware components. It customizes the operating system to a specific computer.

As you probably know, your PC only understands ON and OFF. These conditions are usually represented by the numbers 0 and 1. This unit of information is called a bit. Obviously this amount of information isn't sufficient for any useful computing.

Bits and Bytes Therefore, bits are combined into larger units of information so that larger numbers could be represented.

For example, here is a listing of two-bit numbers:

        00 = 0
        01 = 1
        10 = 2
        11 = 3

This numeric system, which is known as the binary system, is based entirely on the number 2. Therefore, there are only two available values.

The computer industry has adopted the standard of combining eight bits into a *byte*. The following is an example of a few bytes in binary numbers and in their decimal equivalents:

0000 0001	=	1	2^0
0000 0010	=	2	2^1
0001 0001	=	17	2^0+2^4
1000 0000	=	128	2^7
1111 1111	=	255	$2^0+2^1+2^2+2^3+2^4+2^45 2^6+2^7$

From these examples you can see that the largest number that a byte can represent is 255. The number zero (0) can also be represented, which gives us a total of 256 different numbers.

Each letter of the alphabet is replaced by one of these numbers. So, when you press a certain key, the keyboard will send the byte 0110 0001 to the computer, which recognizes this code. Therefore, the "alphabet" used by your computer is limited to 256 characters.

However, there is still a problem. You probably can't decipher the encoded letters. The most important piece of information, the key to our code, is missing. This is fine if the code is supposed to be secret but when the information is supposed to be accessible to everyone, it doesn't work.

ASCII Code   Therefore, the computer industry uses the ASCII (American Standard Code for Information Interchange) code. Actually, this code isn't limited to America but is now internationally accepted. According to the ASCII, the number 97 represents "a", while 65 represents "A". ASCII determines not only letters but also numbers, notation and special characters. The ASCII number 49 represents the number "1" and code number 123 is "{". The first 32 symbols of the ASCII are not printed characters and are used to move the cursor, signal carriage returns or cause the computer to emit a beep.

Many languages such as German, French and Spanish use other characters besides the ones found in the English alphabet. However, there are enough available characters in the ASCII code to include these characters. There are even enough characters available to include graphic symbols. You'll find a complete listing of this character set in Appendix D.

Memory   When your computer system is first started and the DR DOS operating
Management   system is loaded into memory, it reads the CONFIG.SYS file. Since there are so many different PC's, each with a different configuration, DR DOS lets you set up a version of the operating system to suit your requirements. Most of these settings and options deal specifically with your PC's memory management.

DR DOS has a very flexible system for handling memory management. Together, this system is referred to as *MemoryMAX*. Next we'll look at the capabilities of MemoryMAX so that we can intelligently decide which features can provide an optimum use of our PC's memory.

Keep in mind that some of these features can be called upon only when we startup our system. In other words, after DR DOS is fully loaded, these features cannot be altered. Other features however, can be changed after DR DOS is running.

Most of the options are specified by the CONFIG.SYS file. The commands in the CONFIG.SYS file are executed only when the computer is turned on or reset. If you change any of the commands in the CONFIG.SYS file, then you must restart your computer by turning it off and on again or by pressing Ctrl-Alt-Del in order to make the changes effective.

Section 11.1 has more information about changing your CONFIG.SYS file.

9.1   Memory Areas

DR DOS has several capabilities for managing memory. The most important of these are described in this section.

To better understand DR DOS' memory management, you'll have to be familiar with the five major memory areas within your PC. These areas are:

- Conventional or Base memory

- Upper memory

- Extended memory

- High memory

- Expanded memory

We'll explain each of these five areas in this section.

Conventional or Base Memory

Also called base or main memory, conventional memory is the memory area from 0 to 640K. The 640K limit is also known as the 640K barrier. The original IBM PC was designed to use only this area.

A 640K
Barrier
Under DR DOS, the processor can access no more than 640K of main memory. The resident sections of the operating system and installable device drivers are loaded in the lowest part of base memory. The user programs and applications, including the corresponding data, is loaded into the remaining area.

You can't access any more main memory without using special driver software (see the following) which expands the memory management of the operating system. However, you can configure DR DOS to take advantage of special memory areas.

Upper Memory

Since the 8088 and the 8086 processor can only address 1Mb of memory, the memory area between 640K and 1Mb is called upper memory. These 384K of memory are reserved for the video memory, the BIOS system and

143

other expansions such as the BIOS of a hard drive controller or an EGA card.

When the PC was developed, IBM reserved this area for screen cards, BIOS ROM and other expansions and kept the base area memory available for software developers.

RAM and ROM Chips
Specialized add-on cards, such as display adapters, contain ROMs located in the upper memory area. In addition, most AT computers have RAM also located in this same upper memory area. The AT has a mechanism for choosing either ROM or RAM located at the same memory area. Since a program located in ROM executes much slower than a program in RAM, it's desirable to relocate the program from the ROM chips on a display adapter, for example to its corresponding RAM area. This is called shadow RAM.

Shadow RAM reserves room for the temporary storage of ROM information in RAM while your PC is running. DR DOS can store device drivers that usually are stored in base memory in unused upper memory. This gives user programs more memory to use. DR DOS can also store certain parts of the operating system kernal in this memory area.

Extended Memory

PC's with an 80286, 80386 or 80486 processor can address more than 1Mb of memory. The memory above the 1Mb conventional limit is called extended memory. An 80286 processor can address up to 16Mb of memory, while an 80386 or 80486 processor can address up to 4Gb (gigabytes or billion bytes) of memory. Unfortunately, DR DOS cannot automatically use this extended memory.

An AT computer, that is a computer with an 80286 processor, has 640K of conventional memory and an area reserved for the BIOS video and other hardware-dependent devices. The remaining 384K of memory is found in an area above the 1Mb limit. This 384K is part of extended memory.

Real Mode
In order to be compatible with the 8086 and 8088 computers, an AT-class computer operates in *real mode*. In this mode, the computer operates as if it were an 8086 computer and therefore can address a maximum of 1Mb of memory. In real mode, an AT-class computer cannot use memory beyond the 1Mb limit.

Protected Mode   To use memory beyond this 1Mb limit, the processor must be switched to *protected mode*. Again, only 80286, 80386 and 80486 processors are capable of running in protected mode. In this mode, the 1Mb memory limitation is removed. So you can store and retrieve information in memory above the 1Mb limit.

Memory   By itself, DR DOS does not take advantage of protected mode. To be able
Management   to use extended memory, use a memory management program such as
Programs   VDISK.SYS to set up a virtual (RAM) disk or SUPERPCK.EXE to set up a disk cache.

High Memory

The first 64K of extended memory is called high memory or the High Memory Area (HMA). This area can be used only by 80286, 80386 and 80486 processors with more than 1 megabyte of memory installed.

Since DR DOS can move the operating system kernal in this area, it increases the amount of available base memory for your applications. In Section 9.4 we'll discuss how to move the operating system kernal into high memory.

Expanded memory

The Expanded Memory Specification (EMS) is another way to add memory above the 640K barrier. The technique was developed by three leading PC companies: Lotus, Intel and Microsoft. The standard is sometimes referred to as the LIM/EMS standard, a term derived from the initials of these three companies..

EMS is a combination of hardware and software. The memory are chips contained on a printed circuit board with special electronics. One principle behind expanded memory is that it can be used by 8086 and 8088 computers. So memory that uses this scheme must be addressable below the 1Mb limit.

An area in upper memory (between 640K and 1Mb) is designated as a *page frame*. The page frame is a 64K area of memory that acts as a window to a much larger area of expanded memory. The electronic circuitry lets you select the part of expanded memory that appears in this window at any given time. Just as DOS manages memory up to the 640K limit, special software called an EMS driver manages expanded memory. When a program references an area of expanded memory that isn't in the window, the EMS software/hardware combination replaces an unneeded area of memory of the page frame with the area that is needed.

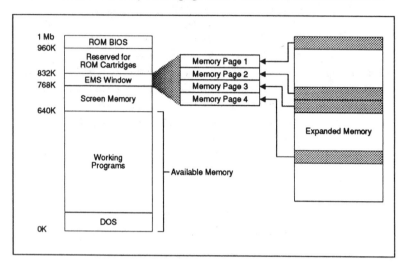

Four pages of extended memory can be placed in the Memory Page Frame. A program called the expanded memory manager controls the assignment of the pages in upper memory when individual pages are being used.

The figure above shows the layout of expanded memory. The expanded memory on the EMS circuit board is completely independent of the computer's conventional memory (and extended memory - if present). The electronic circuitry on the board manages the data in the EMS memory.

Of course a program must be especially written to be able to use expanded memory. But many programs are already set up to recognize and take advantage of a computer's expanded memory. Some of the major applications that can use expanded memory are: dBASE IV, Framework, Lotus 1-2-3, Microsoft Windows, Microsoft Word, Microsoft Works, Turbo Pascal and WordPerfect. There are many other applications that can use expanded memory.

There are several programs which simulate expanded memory entirely in software. With these programs, you do not require a memory expansion board. Instead, the software stores the memory pages that are not being referenced on the hard drive. When these memory pages are later referenced, they are read into memory from the hard drive. Simulating expanded memory in this way requires more time than using an expanded memory board to access the memory pages from the hard drive, but may be an economical solution if the additional processing time is not a concern.

Utility Programs for expanded memory

The DR DOS 6.0 device driver EMM386.SYS is used by 80386 and 80486 processors to convert extended memory into expanded memory. This driver makes extended memory function according to the LIM/EMS standard. EMM386.SYS has other capabilities as well. Upper memory between 640K and 1Mb that isn't being used by DR DOS can be used to store other device driver programs and many Terminate and Stay Resident (TSR) programs using the HILOAD command. By moving these programs into high memory, additional conventional memory is freed up for other applications.

Another DR DOS 6.0 device driver EMMXMA.SYS is used by computers with memory cards compatible with the IBM XMA standard to convert extended memory to expanded memory.

9.2 Displaying Memory

You can get an overview of the organization of your computer's memory with the MEM command:

MEM (Enter)

This shows information on the amount of conventional memory, the largest available block and amount (if any) of extended memory.

Switches you can use with MEM include:

/H	Shows help information.
/B	Displays the areas of memory which are used by different parts of the operating system.
/D	Displays information on the loadable device drivers including their location in memory.
/S	Displays the DOS disk buffer chain.
/P	Pauses the display when the screen is full. Strike (press) any key to continue the display.
/M	Provides a graphic display for the location of RAM, ROM and EMS memory.
/A	Shows all of the above information.

You can receive complete memory information using the MEM command. The /A switch graphically displays detailed information on your PC's memory configuration. This is usually so much information that we recommend using the /P switch to pause at every full screen of information. For example, type the following command:

MEM /A/P (Enter)

This command displays the following (your system will differ, depending on the memory configuration):

```
 ┌ Address ──┬─ Owner ──┬─ Size ──────────┬─ Type ────────────────────────┐
 │   0:0000   │ -------- │ A0000h,  655,360 │ ------------- RAM -------------- │
 ├────────────┼──────────┼──────────────────┼────────────────────────────────┤
 │   0:0000   │ -------- │   400h,    1,024 │ Interrupt vectors             │
 │  40:0000   │ -------- │   100h,      256 │ ROM BIOS data area            │
 │  50:0000   │ DR DOS   │   200h,      512 │ DOS data area                 │
 │  70:0000   │ DR BIOS  │   B20h,    2,848 │ Device drivers                │
 │  70:050B   │ PRN      │                  │ Built-in device driver        │
 │  70:051D   │ LPT1     │                  │ Built-in device driver        │
 │  70:052F   │ LPT2     │                  │ Built-in device driver        │
 │  70:0541   │ LPT3     │                  │ Built-in device driver        │
 │  70:0553   │ AUX      │                  │ Built-in device driver        │
 │  70:0565   │ COM1     │                  │ Built-in device driver        │
 │  70:0577   │ COM2     │                  │ Built-in device driver        │
 │  70:0589   │ COM3     │                  │ Built-in device driver        │
 │  70:059B   │ COM4     │                  │ Built-in device driver        │
 │  70:0602   │ CLOCK$   │                  │ Built-in device driver        │
 │  70:0645   │ CON      │                  │ Built-in device driver        │
 │  70:0671   │ A:-C:    │                  │ Built-in device driver        │
 │ 122:0000   │ DR DOS   │  11B0h,    4,528 │ System                        │
 │ 122:0048   │ NUL      │                  │ Built-in device driver        │
 │ 23D:0000   │ DR DOS   │  16B10h,  92,944 │ System                        │
 │ 24F:0000   │ D:       │  ACEOh,   44,256 │ Loadable device driver        │
 │ D5D:0000   │ DR DOS   │  1000h,    4,096 │ 8 Disk buffers                │
 │more...     │          │                  │                                │
 │ DB9:15C0   │ DR DOS   │   DEOh,    3,552 │ DR DOS BIOS code              │
 │ CF3:3000   │ DR DOS   │  9440h,   37,952 │ DR DOS kernel code            │
 │ 18EE:0000  │ COMMAND  │  1590h,    5,520 │ Program                       │
 │ 1A47:0000  │ COMMAND  │   110h,      272 │ Environment                   │
 │ 1A58:0000  │ MEM      │    80h,      128 │ Environment                   │
 │ 1A60:0000  │ MEM      │  13AD0h,  80,592 │ Program                       │
 │ 2E0D:0000  │ -------- │  71F30h, 466,736 │ FREE                          │
 ├────────────┼──────────┼──────────────────┼────────────────────────────────┤
 │ C000:0000  │ -------- │  4000h,   16,384 │ ------------- ROM -------------- │
 │ E000:0000  │ -------- │ 20000h,  131,072 │ ------------- ROM -------------- │
 └────────────┴──────────┴──────────────────┴────────────────────────────────┘
more...
```

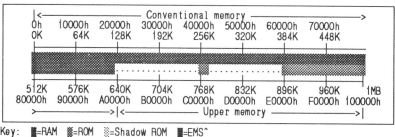

```
Key:  ▓=RAM  ▨=ROM  ░=Shadow ROM  ■=EMS^
┌─ Memory Type ──────┬─── Total Bytes ( Kbytes  ) ─┬──── Available ────┐
│ Conventional       │    655,360 (    640K )      │   547,440 (   534K ) │
│ Extended           │  1,048,576 (  1,024K )      │ 1,048,576 ( 1,024K ) │
└────────────────────┴─────────────────────────────┴─────────────────────┘
```

Complete memory contents displayed using the MEM command with the /A and /P switches

9.3 Starting The System

In order to take better advantage of DR DOS' memory management features, lets see how DR DOS gets things going on your computer at start up.

When your computer is started (or restarted), a section of conventional memory is reserved by DR DOS and cannot be used by you or your applications. In this reserved area, DR DOS stores information in several tables and data areas. Then two files are copied from the boot disk into memory - the files IBMBIO.COM and IBMDOS.COM. These two files are the programs that serve as the interface between the COMMAND.COM command interpreter, the computer hardware and the BIOS (Binary Input/Output System). IBMBIO.COM and IBMDOS.COM are part of the operating system kernal. Next the device drivers and the resident portion of COMMAND.COM are read into memory.

Resident and transient commands
The command interpreter is divided into a resident and a transient portion. The resident portion is stored in low conventional memory and the transient portion in the upper end of conventional memory. By dividing it into two portions, the memory occupied by the transient portion can be used by other programs if it is required. After a user program ends and returns control to the resident portion of the command interpreter, DR DOS checks to see if the transient section was overwritten. If so, a fresh copy of the transient section is reread from the boot disk.

A section of conventional memory called the environment area immediately follows the resident portion of the command interpreter. This size of this area can be defined up to 32K and is also set at start up.

The organization of the lowest area of conventional memory is determined at start up and cannot be changed. However, the commands in the CONFIG.SYS file can be used to alter the layout and contents of conventional memory.

The MEM command can be used to view the lowest area of conventional memory. The /B switch displays the areas of memory which are used by different parts of the operating system.

Address	Owner	Size		Type
0:0000	--------	400h,	1,024	Interrupt vectors
40:0000	--------	100h,	256	ROM BIOS data area
50:0000	DR DOS	200h,	512	DOS data area
70:0000	DR BIOS	B20h,	2,848	Device drivers
122:0000	DR DOS	11B0h,	4,528	System
23D:0000	DR DOS	16B10h,	92,944	System
D5D:0000	DR DOS	1000h,	4,096	8 Disk buffers
DB9:15C0	DR DOS	DE0h,	3,552	DR DOS BIOS code
CF3:3000	DR DOS	9440h,	37,952	DR DOS kernel code
18EE:0000	COMMAND	1590h,	5,520	Program
1A47:0000	COMMAND	110h,	272	Environment
1A58:0000	MEM	80h,	128	Environment
1A60:0000	MEM	13AD0h,	80,592	Program
2E0D:0000	--------	71F30h,	466,736	FREE

Memory contents of conventional memory displayed using the MEM command with the /B switch

9.4   HIDOS.SYS

If you have a 80286 processor and extended memory, you can move most of the DR DOS operating system kernal out of conventional memory and into the high memory area (the first 64K of memory beginning at 1Mb). You can also relocate TSR's and other device driver into upper memory (beginning at 640K and extending to 1Mb). For these functions, you use the HIDOS.SYS device driver.

The simplest way to install the memory management drivers is to do it automatically from the SETUP program. However, this section will show you alternative ways to use HIDOS.SYS

Moving the
kernal

By including the HIDOS.SYS driver in your CONFIG.SYS file, you can move the kernal into the high memory area. The statement like this in your CONFIG.SYS file performs the relocation:

```
DEVICE = C\DRDOS\HIDOS.SYS
```

There are many options that can be added to this statement, many of which are too detailed to describe here. See the DR DOS DOSBOOK program for complete information on HIDOS.SYS. But we'll look at a few of them so that you can be familiar with the possibilities:

/AUTOSCAN=start-end	Scans an area of high memory to see if it is usable. The default areas are C000H for the starting area and FFFFH for the ending area.
/EXCLUDE=start-end	To exclude a portion of high memory which otherwise is useable.
/INCLUDE=start-end	Includes a portion of high memory which otherwise is ignored.
/VIDEO[=[*start*]-*end*]	Releases unused space in upper memory that is reserved for the Video Display Adapter.
/USE=start-end	Similar to /INCLUDE but overrides all memory tests and makes available all upper memory which you specify.
/ROM=start-end	Copies slow ROM into fast ROM.
/ROM=AUTO	Copies all ROM in upper memory to RAM.

To relocate the DR DOS kernal for applications to use:

B/DOS=AUTO   Scans upper memory for a contiguous area of
                              37K in which to place the kernal.

B/DOS=FFFF   Relocates the kernal to segment FFFF in high
                              memory.

B/DOS=nnnn   Relocates the kernal to a specific (nnnn)
                              address in upper memory. Make certain that a
                              contiguous area of 37K is available at location
                              nnnn.

9.5   EMM386.SYS

EMM386.SYS is a DR DOS device driver which manages expanded and extended memory. As its name might suggest, the EMM386.SYS device driver requires that you have a 80386 (or the more advanced 80486) processor.

One important function of EMM386.SYS is to relocate the DR DOS operating system kernal to high or upper memory. Another function of EMM386.SYS is to emulate LIM/EMS expanded memory. Still another function of EMM386.SYS is to prepare upper memory for relocating TSRs and other device drivers from conventional memory with the HILOAD, HIINSTALL and HIDEVICE commands.

Configuring   By including EMM386.SYS in your CONFIG.SYS file, you can take
EMM386.SYS   advantage of these and other memory features:

```
DEVICE = C:\DRDOS\EMM386.SYS
```

As with the HIDOS.SYS device driver, EMM386.SYS offers many possibilities for customizing your computer for your particular requirements. See the DR DOS DOSBOOK program for complete information on EMM386.SYS. Here are a few of the options:

To control LIM 4.0 emulation:

/FRAME=AUTO   Searches through upper memory for a free 64K window (default).

/FRAME=NONE   Use this option to use the advantages of EMM386.SYS without using expanded memory on your PC.

/FRAME=nnnn   Specifies an address for the location of the 64K byte window.

To control the amount of memory you want for LIM/EMS:

/KB = 0   Use all extended memory.

/KB = nnnn   Use the specified amount of memory.

To relocate the DR DOS kernal for applications to use:

B/DOS=AUTO
: To scan upper memory for a contiguous area of 37K in which to place the kernal.

B/DOS=FFFF
: To relocate the kernal to segment FFFF in high memory.

B/DOS=nnnn
: To relocate the kernal to a specific (nnnn) address in upper memory. Make certain that a contiguous area of 37K is available at location nnnn.

Other commands available include:

/AUTOSCAN=start-end
: To scan an area of upper memory to see if it is usable.

/INCLUDE=start-end
: To include a portion of upper memory which otherwise is ignored.

/EXCLUDE=start-end
: To exclude a portion of upper memory which otherwise is useable.

/VIDEO[=[*start*]-*end*]
: Releases unused space in upper memory that is reserved for the Video Display Adapter.

9.6   EMMXMA.SYS

EMMXMA.SYS is another DR DOS device driver which converts extended memory into LIM compatible expanded memory, but only for IBM PS/2 computers with memory boards compatible with the IBM XMA standard.

This device driver is hardware specific and by default creates an expanded memory page frame between C000H and DFFFH. You can specify the amount of memory to be converted to expanded memory.

To install this device driver for 2MB of expanded memory, use the following in your CONFIG.SYS file:

```
DEVICE = C:\DRDOS\EMMXMA.SYS /KB=2048
```

Here are the options:

/FRAME=xxxx   Specifies the hexadecimal segment address of the start of the 64K byte window. If this option is omitted, EMMXMA.SYS automatically searches for a free 64K window.

/KB=ddd   Specifies (ddd) amount of memory you want to allocate for LIM memory.

10. Special Utility Programs

10. Special Utility Programs

We'll discuss various DR DOS utility programs in this chapter.

- EDITOR (Section 10.1) is a convenient full-screen editor which uses WordStar key commands.

- PASSWORD (Section 10.2) allows you to protect a file from unauthorized use.

- Security (Section 10.3) lets you protect your system from unauthorized access.

- FILELINK (Section 10.4) allows you to transfer files between computers, over serial cables.

- TOUCH (Section 10.5) allows you to change the creation dates for one or more files.

- CURSOR (Section 10.6) allows you to change the flash interval and appearance of the cursor.

- DOSBOOK (Section 10.7) is a complete on-line reference to DR DOS. Entering HELP at the DOS prompt will also load the DOSBOOK program.

10.1 EDITOR

You can use the editor to create, view or change ASCII text files while in DR DOS. This simple yet functional text editor has several basic commands and you can use it instead of a full-fledged word processor.

For example, you can use the EDITOR if you want to change the AUTOEXEC.BAT file. The commands of the EDITOR are specified using [Ctrl] key combinations similar to those used by the Wordstar word processor.

Starting   There are two ways to start EDITOR:

1. For editing a new file.

2. For editing an existing file.

To start the EDITOR on a new file, type the following:

EDITOR (Enter)

The following startup message of the editor appears on the screen prompting you to enter a filename.

```
              EDITOR R2.00     Full Screen Text Editor
   Copyright (c) 1988,1989,1990 Digital Research Inc. All rights reserved.




   Please enter the name of the text file you wish to edit.
   If the file does not already exist it will be created.
   Press the Esc key to leave this program.

   File name?
```

If you don't enter a filename and press either (Enter) or (Esc), you'll exit the EDITOR and return to the DR DOS prompt.

Entering   Type in the filename you want to use and press the (Enter) key. If a file
Filenames   with this name does not exist, the editor asks if you want to create a new
                file using this name. Press (Y) to create the file or press the (N) key to
                return to the startup screen of the editor. Then you can enter another
                filename.

You can exit EDITOR at any time while entering a filename by pressing (Esc).

If a file with this name exists, EDITOR displays the file on the screen.

To edit an existing filename or create a new file immediately, type the following:

EDITOR test.txt (Enter)

If the file TEST.TXT already exists, the contents are displayed on the screen. You can then begin editing the file.

Creating a
File
If the file does not exist, a message appears saying that the file was not found. EDITOR asks if you want to create a new file. Press Ⓨ to create the file.

The following screen then appears:

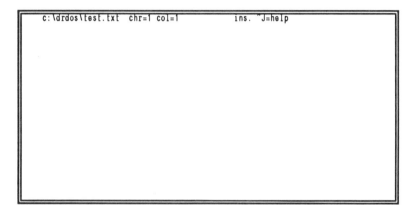

```
c:\drdos\test.txt  chr=1 col=1           ins.  ^J=help
```

If you answer with Ⓝ, you're returned to the startup screen of the editor. You can then enter another filename.

Need Help?
After the EDITOR switches to the editing screen, you can display different screens of help information by pressing ⁅F1⁆ or ⁅Ctrl⁆+⁅J⁆.

```
Entering text

    Type text as at a typewriter. Press the Enter key to begin a new line.
    In insert mode existing text is moved aside to accommodate text you type.
    In overwrite mode the text you type replaces existing text.

    Ctrl-V   Switch between insert and overwrite modes
    Ctrl-N   Insert new line at cursor
    Ctrl-P   The next character you type is entered as a control code
    Ctrl-Qn  Enter character code directly (0..255 or 0x00..0xFF)

Deleting text

    Ctrl-H   Delete the character immediately before the cursor
    Ctrl-G   Delete the character at the cursor
    Ctrl-T   Delete the "word" at the cursor
    Ctrl-Y   Delete the line containing the cursor



Press Enter for next page, or Esc to resume editing...
```

161

Press (Enter) to page through the help screens. After the last page of the help screen, the following prompt appears:

```
Do you wish to have the quick reference display (Y/N)?
```

Press (Y) to keep the quick reference display visible on the editing screen or press (N) to remove it.

Cursor   Move the cursor by using the arrow keys or (PgUp), (PgDn), (Home) or
Movement   (End). There are also corresponding key combinations using (Ctrl):

(Ctrl)+(D)	Moves the cursor one position to the right.
(Ctrl)+(S)	Moves the cursor one position to the left.
(Ctrl)+(E)	Moves the cursor up one line.
(Ctrl)+(X)	Moves the cursor down one line.
(Ctrl)+(R)	Moves the cursor back one page.
(Ctrl)+(C)	Moves the cursor forward one page.
(Ctrl)+(Q)(S)	Moves the cursor to the beginning of the line.
(Ctrl)+(Q)(D)	Moves the cursor to the end of the line.

You can also move the cursor with the following (Ctrl) combinations:

(Ctrl)+(F)	Moves the cursor one word to the right.
(Ctrl)+(A)	Moves the cursor one word to the left.
(Ctrl)+(Q)(R)	Moves the cursor to the beginning of the text.
(Ctrl)+(Q)(C)	Moves the cursor to the end of the text.
(Ctrl)+(Q)(B)	Moves the cursor to the beginning of a block.
(Ctrl)+(Q)(K)	Moves the cursor to the end of a block.

Erasing   Entering text is done just as you would on a normal typewriter. Erasing
Characters   individual characters is done with (Del) (erasing the character at the cursor position) or with (Backspace) (erasing the character preceding the cursor).

Press the (Ins) key to switch between overwrite and insert modes. The (Ctrl)+(Y) combination erases the entire line of text on which the cursor is positioned.

Blocks   A block is any number of successive characters, words or lines of text. You can move, copy, erase, and save a block. A block can be reread from disks and inserted at the cursor position.

To work with a block, you must first mark the text which makes up the block.

Marking
Blocks

Position the cursor to the start of the text that you want to process with the block commands and press [Ctrl]+[K][B]. The "B" character then appears at this location. Move the cursor to the end of the section of text and press [Ctrl]+[K][K]. The character "K" appears here. The block becomes highlighted.

You can now move, copy or delete this block.

There is a small trick you can use in remembering most of the EDITOR block commands. Remember that [Ctrl]+[K] chooses a block command and the word "block" ends with "K". The second letter usually corresponds to the command. You'll see how on the next page.

Moving a
Block

First move the cursor to the new position where you're moving the block. Then press [Ctrl]+[K][V]. The marked block will now appear at the new position.

Copying
Blocks

A copy of the marked block is done with [Ctrl]+[K][C]. The "C" is similar to the DR DOS COPY command and is therefore easy to remember.

Erasing Blocks

Delete a marked block by pressing [Ctrl]+[K][Y]. As you know, the "Y" erases a single line of text. The same principle applies here to blocks.

Writing Blocks

If you want to insert a selection of text from one file to a second file, you must first write the block to disk. Then you can edit the second file and read the block back from disk.

A block that has been marked is written to disk using the [Ctrl]+[K][W] key combination. The "W" represents "write". You must enter a filename for the block.

Reading Blocks

To reread a block that has been written to disk, use [Ctrl]+[K][R]. The "R" represents "read". You must enter the block's filename. The block is then inserted at the cursor position.

Ending

There are three ways to leave the EDITOR:

1. If you want to save the text to disk and leave the editor, press the `Ctrl`+`K``X` key combination. It returns to the DR DOS prompt.

2. If you want to save the text to disk and return to the EDITOR startup screen, press the `Ctrl`+`K``Q` key combination. You then have the opportunity to edit another file. You can recall the name of the file that was processed last with `Ctrl`+`R` and continue editing this file.

3. If you want to exit the EDITOR without saving changes or the file, press the `Ctrl`+`K``Q` key combination. The EDITOR displays:

    ```
    Abandon changes to test file (Y/N)
    ```

    If you want to save the changes, press `N` and follow Step 1 or Step 2 above. If you press `Y` you're returned to the EDITOR startup screen.

10.2 PASSWORD

DR DOS also has a way to prevent unauthorized access to files and directories. You can assign a password to files and directories that must be entered before a user can access those files and directories. A password can have a maximum of eight characters.

There are up to three password combinations for files and one for directories.

Entering
Passwords

If you want to protect files from unauthorized reading, copying, deleting, renaming, changing attributes or modifying, use the /R switch and a password. We're using TOM as the password in the following example:

```
PASSWORD TEST.TXT /R:TOM (Enter)
```

To experiment with this simple example of the PASSWORD command, try loading the TEST.TXT into EDITOR.

DR DOS will respond with:

```
Disk Error - Invalid password
File - c:\test.txt

Press Esc to continue
```

If you try the COPY command on the TEST.TXT file by typing:

```
COPY TEXT.TXT PROBE.TXT
```

DR DOS displays the following error message:

```
Invalid Password
```

To modify TEST.TXT, you must include the password "TOM". To copy the TEST.TXT file, separate the password with a semicolon:

```
COPY TEST.TXT;TOM PROBE.TXT (Enter)
```

/W Switch

In the following example, a user can read and copy a file without a password, but cannot write to, delete, rename or otherwise modify the file TEXT.TXT file:

PASSWORD TEXT.TXT /W:JOE (Enter)

The /W switch allows anyone to perform an operation which reads the file as long as that operation does not change any of the file's attributes. So anyone can use the following copy command:

COPY TEST.TXT PROBE.TXT

The above copy operation does not change the protected file TEST.TXT. However, the following operation requires the user to enter the correct password to modify the protected file:

COPY PROBE.TXT TEST.TXT

The copied file is not protected by the password.

/D Switch   You can also protect files from renaming and deletion. This is done with the /D option:

PASSWORD TEST.TXT /D:HARRY

Entering Directory Passwords

Protecting   A password can be specified for directories with the /P option. "P"
Directories   represents the word "path".

The directory "C:\DOC\BOOK" is protected by a password with the following command:

PASSWORD C:\DOC\BOOK /P:TOM

Directories are automatically protected from reading, writing and deletion. Users are prompted for a password each time the directory is accessed.

Entering Passwords

Global   When using DR DOS operations on protected files or directories, you
Password   must separate the password from the filename by a semicolon when attempting to access a protected file. This can make everyday work very slow, there is a way to enter a global password.

A global password allows you to use all DR DOS protected files which are set to this password without entering the password. For example, if you have protected a text file from being read and want to use this file from a word processor, you must either cancel the password or give it a global password. A global password is given with the /G switch.

In our example:

```
PASSWORD /G:TOM
```

The global password can be canceled with the /NG option:

```
PASSWORD /NG
```

After this command is specified, the password "TOM" must be entered for all protected files.

Removing Passwords

Remove passwords from files with the /N switch. For example, to remove the TOM password from the TEST.TXT file, enter the following:

```
PASSWORD TEXT.TXT;TOM /N  (Enter)
```

You must use the /NP switch for directories:

```
PASSWORD C:\TEXTS\BOOK;TOM /NP  (Enter)
```

/R:password	Protects the file attributes from reading, writing, copying, deletion, renaming and modification.
/W:password	Protects the file attributes from users overwriting, copying, deletion, renaming and modifying them.
/D:password	Protects the file from renaming and deletion.
/N	Removes passwords from files.
/C:\DIRECTORY /P:password	Protects directories from reading, writing and deletion.
/NP:password	Removes passwords from directories.
/G:password	Creates a global password.
/NG:password	Removes the global password.

10.3 Security

Besides the security provided by the PASSWORD command, DR DOS 6.0 offers a *Security* option. When this option is installed, it prevents unauthorized users from accessing your computer.

This system prevents both casual and unauthorized access to your computer. It will also prevent a user from gaining access to your computer by booting from a floppy disk.

Warning!!

> **CAUTION!!!!**
>
> If you intend to install System Security, make absolutely certain that you remember your password and enter the password properly. Even DR DOS cannot be reinstalled on a password protected disk. A lost password means that your system is locked, permanently.
>
> Your only alternative will be to reformat your disk drive, eliminating all data on the drive.
>
> To compound your problems, you cannot reboot with a DR DOS disk and use the DR DOS FDISK command. It will be necessary to obtain a boot disk from some other operating system, such as MS-DOS and FDISK from that operating system, then attempt to reboot with DR DOS and use the DR DOS FDISK command to repartition your hard drive.
>
> Of course, this process will totally and permanently destroy all data on your hard disk.

Security is provided on two levels: locking all fixed disks to prevent access by another operating system booted from a floppy disk, and password protection for logging in for day to day usage.

The Master Key

The master key locks all fixed disks to prevent access by another operating system booted from a floppy disk.

This is an automatic feature and is done if you select Security from the SETUP.

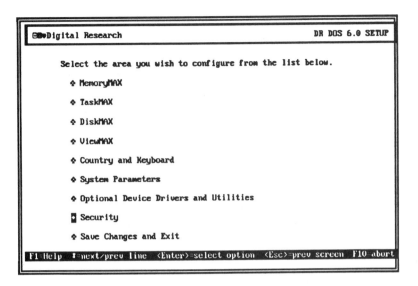

Preparing to install Security from SETUP

Select *Security* from the Configuration menu, and press (Enter). A screen will be displayed requesting confirmation that you intend to enable security.

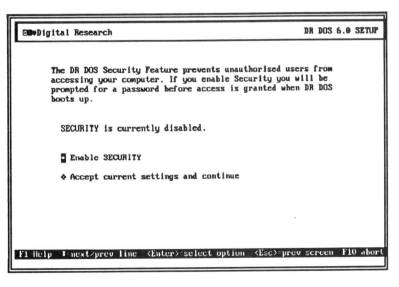

Enabling Security

Next, you will be asked to provide a password which will be required if you ever want to disable Security. Enter any password, up to 12 alphanumeric characters. Make sure that you keep this master password secret and stored in a safe place. It is the only way you can disable the Security feature.

SETUP will confirm your choice of a master password by asking you to enter it twice. Both passwords entered must be identical to be accepted.

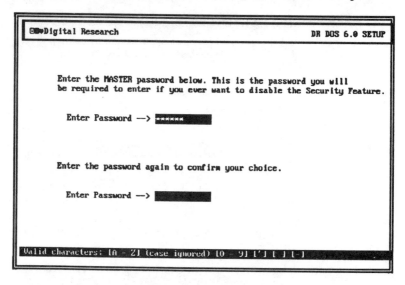

Entering the Master Password

Next, you will be asked to select and enter a user password. This is your key for logging in for daily activity and will be required every time you boot your computer. This password can be changed anytime from SETUP and should be changed regularly for security.

Again, you will be asked to enter the selected password twice to confirm it was entered correctly.

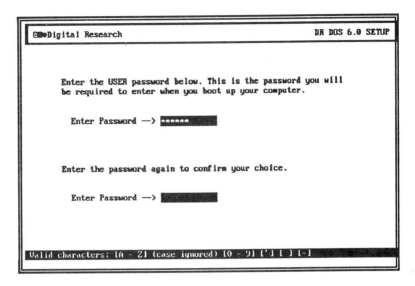

Entering and confirming the User Password

Save the new configuration files. SETUP will update your CONFIG.SYS file to include LOGIN.

Reboot your computer to register the changes made to your CONFIG.SYS file.

You will be prompted for your password every time your computer is booted.

The login screen may be customized by modifying the file LOGIN.TXT, located in your DRDOS directory.

Remember to keep both your Master and User passwords in a safe, secure location. Remember, without the proper password, even you can't access your computer system.

10.4 FILELINK

DR DOS has the capability of exchanging files between computers using an RS232 null modem cable connected to the serial ports of each computer. This is very useful for exchanging files between computers that use different diskette formats. For example, the files between a laptop computer with a 3.5" disk drive and a desktop computer with only a 5.25" disk drive (or no disk drive).

If one of the computers is a notebook PC, which may not even have a disk drive, data transfer using the serial interface is an absolute necessity.

A null modem cable connects the two computers together to allow FILELINK to transfer files between the computers. A special data transfer cable for FILELINK is available from Abacus, please see the ads in the back of this book for more information about ordering the FILELINK compatible Universal Data Transfer cable.

Since a null modem cable is a specially configured serial cable, you do not need to use a modem. The null modem cable must match each of the computers which you plan to link with FILELINK. Most serial ports on PCs have either 9-pin or 25-pin D-type male connectors, so the null modem cable you use must be a 9-pin or 25-pin D-type female connector.

The following are several important terms we'll use in this section:

Baud rate	Gives the transfer speed of data in bits per second.
COM1:	Refer to communication port #1.
COM2:	Refer to communication port #2.
Master	Refers to the computer on which the commands are typed.
Parity bit	Adds an extra bit to a data word for parity checking.
Slave	Refers to the computer that will be controlled. The peripherals of the slave computer are used by the master computer.
Stop bit	A bit which informs the slave computer that data transmission is complete.

Setting the Parameters for FILELINK

Installing
FILELINK

FILELINK requires parameters in order to establish correct connection between the two computers. You enter the parameters with each FILELINK command, but only one parameter at a time should be specified.

To specify the serial interface and transfer speed, use the FILELINK SETUP command:

```
FILELINK SETUP <parameters> Enter
```

Parameters for
FILELINK
SETUP

Normally you'll use either COM1: or COM2: for the communication interface. Following the communication interface, next specify the baud rate. This is the transfer speed of the data between the two computers. The baud rate indicates how many bits per second should be sent through the cable. The bits are sent one after another in a serial transfer. A parity bit and one or two stop bits come with the eight bits of a data byte.

For an example, if you want to specify a baud rate of 38,400 baud in FILELINK using the first serial interface, type the following command:

```
FILELINK SETUP COM1:38 Enter
```

The baud rate must be the same for each computer. You only need to specify the first two numbers of the baud rate in the command. DR DOS uses these abbreviations for the baud rates:

Baud rate	Abbreviation
110	11
150	15
300	30
600	60
1200	12
2400	24
4800	48
9600	96
19,200	19
38,400	38
56,700	57
115,200	115

FILELINK stores these parameters in the FILELINK.CFG file. If you use FILELINK SETUP again, the parameters are read from this file and do not have to be re-entered.

Installing FILELINK on the Slave Computer

To work with FILELINK, the program must be running on the master and slave computers, although you need to start FILELINK on only one computer. Then transfer the program to the second computer over the serial interface. Start FILELINK by typing:

```
FILELINK DUPLICATE [Enter]
```

Master and Slave

The computer on which the FILELINK commands are typed is called the "master". The second computer is the "slave".

FILELINK prompts you to enter the COM port (1 or 2) over which the connection to the remote computers is to be made. If you press [1], FILELINK prompts you to enter the following two lines on the slave computer:

```
MODE COM1:9600,N,8,1,P
CTTY COM1:
```

The first command initializes the first serial interface on the slave with the following data:

9600	Transfer rate
N	No parity
8	Number of data bits
1	Stop bit
P	Instructs the computer to wait for a connection

DR DOS displays an error message if you don't enter the above parameters.

CTTY	Redirects keyboard and screen data channels to COM1:.
COM1	Refers to serial port #1.

CTTY is similar to piping with ">" and "<" except that piping is not limited to one command. That means the data channel remains in effect until the CTTY CON: command is received over the serial interface which restores the normal assignment.

Connection Press (Enter) on the master computer after you have prepared the slave computer to accept the connection. FILELINK now attempts to make a connection. If the connection is successful, a loading program and batch file are transferred to the slave computer.

FILELINK then starts the batch file from the master. This restores the normal assignment of keyboard and screen on the slave with CTTY CON:. The load program is then started.

FILELINK sends a copy of itself and a configuration file over the interface to the slave. If FILELINK is received on the slave without an error, the loading program is erased because it is no longer needed.

Look at the messages on the screen of the slave computer.

These operations are done at a baud rate of 9600, not at the speed set in the SETUP. This is done because not all computers work at the higher baud rates. If one of the two computers was not able to transfer at 38400 baud, FILELINK could not have made the connection.

Since the connection is made at only 9600 baud, this is a test to see if the devices are connected correctly. After the connection is made they switch to the higher speed, if possible. You can recognize this in the command line displayed on the slave computer:

```
FILELINK SET COM1:38400
```

Running FILELINK

Alternatively, DR DOS 6.0 can be installed on the remote computer, or a copy of the FILELINK command may be placed on it. Enter the following command at the system prompt of the remote computer to place it in Slave mode:

```
FILELINK SLAVE
```

Now, type the following command line on your Master computer to start FILELINK with the menu interface.

```
FILELINK
```

175

Overview of the FILELINK Commands

Here are the FILELINK commands and their abbreviations:

Command	Abbreviation
DIRECTORY	DIR
DUPLICATE	DUP
QUIT	QUI
RECEIVE	REC
SETUP	SET
SLAVE	SLA
TRANSMIT	TRA

Setting the Slave Mode

The last command line that appears on the Slave computer's screen reads:

`FILELINK SLA`

This sets the computer to Slave mode.

Ending the Slave Mode

Pressing Ctrl+C exits Slave mode. The following exits Slave mode from the Master computer:

`FILELINK QUIT` Enter

Displaying the Directory

To display the directory of the Slave computer on the Master computer, the DIRECTORY command is used.

`FILELINK DIRECTORY` Enter

The following switches are available for this command:

/A	Displays files whose archive bit is set.
/D:DATE	Displays files changed since the given date.
/H	Displays hidden files.
/S	Displays system files.
/P	Displays the files one screen at a time.

For example, the following command shows you the files whose archive bit is set and stops the output after each screen page.

```
FILELINK DIRECTORY/A/P Enter
```

Sending Files

Transferring files from the master computer to the slave computer is done with the "FILELINK TRANSMIT" command. The following switches apply to the TRANSMIT command:

/A	Copies only files whose archive bit is set.
/D:DATE	Copies only files changed since the given date.
/H	Copies hidden files and system files.
/M	Copies only files whose archive bit is set and that do not exist on the target drive or exist with an erased archive bit.
/P	Waits for a key to be pressed for each file.
/R	Overwrites read-only files on the target drive.
/S	Copies the subdirectories of the given path.
/U	Copies files that do not exist on the target drive or that are newer than the files on the target drive.

For example, this command copies all of the files from the C:\TEXTS directory of the master computer into the C:BOOK directory of the slave.

```
FILELINK TRANSMIT C:\TEXTS C:\BOOK Enter
```

Receiving Files

The master can receive files from the slave with the FILELINK RECEIVE command.

The following command copies the directory "C:\DRBOOK" from the slave computer to the "D:\DRBOOK" directory on the master computer.

```
FILELINK RECEIVE C:\DRBOOK D:\DRBOOK Enter
```

The same switches that were used for TRANSMIT can be used for RECEIVE.

177

10.5 TOUCH

Have you ever noticed that dozens of files that comprise many commercial software packages all have the same creation date and time?

You can change the creation date and time of any file or all files by using TOUCH. The following command changes the creation date and time for every file in your hard disk to the current date and time in your PC:

TOUCH *.* (Enter)

You can also use switches to specify a certain creation date and time. This would allow you to determine which entries to change and whether to change files from subdirectories:

/D:mm-dd-yy	Determines the date for the entries.
/P	You confirm if each entry is to change by pressing (Y) or (N).
/R	Changes files which are read-only.
/S	Changes files in the subdirectories of the current directory.
/F:[E|J|U]	Specifies European, Japanese or USA date format (see note below).
/T:hh:mm:ss	Determines the time for the entries.

Note: The format of the date corresponds to the country code that is specified in the CONFIG.SYS file. This country code can be overwritten with the /F:[E|J|U] switch.

Type the following to change the date and time for all .TXT files (you can substitute another date and time):

TOUCH *.TXT /D:01-10-90 /T:12:00 (Enter)

Type the following to change the files of the subdirectories of the current directory:

TOUCH *.DAT /S (Enter)

Type the following to change the date and time for every file (you can confirm if the date and time will change for each file):

TOUCH *.* /D:01-10-90 /T:12:00 /P (Enter)

10.6 CURSOR

The cursor is difficult to see on certain monitors, this is especially true with the LCD screens of many laptop computers. To change the rate at which the cursor blinks you can use the CURSOR command.

The CURSOR command serves two very practical and useful functions:

1. Use the CURSOR command to set the frequency of the flash interval in multiples of a twentieth of a second.

2. The appearance of the cursor changes from the hardware cursor (small blinking line) to a large flashing block. This is very visible on LCD screens.

If you wanted to change the flash interval so that the cursor flashes every 8/20 (4/10) of a second, type the following:

CURSOR /S8 [Enter]

You can use values between 1 and 20, with 1 representing the fastest flash. A value of four is the default if you do not enter a value.

To eliminate the snow that occurs on many CGA monitors and set the flash interval to 10/20 (1/2) of a second, type the following:

CURSOR /S10 /C [Enter]

To turn off the software cursor, type the following:

CURSOR OFF [Enter]

10.7 DOSBOOK

DOSBOOK is a complete hypertext on-line reference to DR DOS. This is one of the best features of DR DOS, instructions for all the DOS commands and functions can be accessed at any time. DOSBOOK contains a complete description of the DR DOS basics, all commands and functions and help when troubleshooting DR DOS.

Enter DOSBOOK at the DOS prompt and the DOSBOOK welcome screen will be displayed. You can also enter HELP to load the DOSBOOK program, the DRDOS directory contains a HELP.BAT file which call the DOSBOOK program. Once the DOSBOOK program is loaded, press F1 and the instructions for using the DOSBOOK program will be displayed.

Entering DOSBOOK followed by the name of a command will display the information about the command. The DOSBOOK program has two menus, Window and Help:

Window

Resize Window	Toggles the window between the full screen an a smaller window.
Print Section	Allows you to print the current topic.
Exit, retain Window	Keeps the displayed instructions on the screen, above the command line when you exit the DOS BOOK program.
Exit	Exits DOSBOOK and clears the screen.

Help

Help for DOSBOOK	Displays instructions for using the DOSBOOK program.
Contents	Displays the contents for DOSBOOK.
Glossary	Displays a list of computer terms, select the term and press Enter for a definition of the term.
Index	Displays the subject index.
Backtrack	Displays last topic viewed.
Next	Displays the next page in the DOSBOOK. This can be used to page thru the Glossary.
Previous	Displays the previous page in the DOSBOOK.
About	Displays the copyright screen for the DOSBOOK program.

11. Fine Tuning DR DOS

11. Fine Tuning DR DOS

In this chapter we'll discuss how you can "fine tune" your PC so that DR DOS and your applications will run more efficiently. Even though the SETUP program greatly simplifies installing DR DOS and managing your memory efficiently, some things can be improved.

For information on fine tuning memory and memory management, refer to Chapter 9.

11.1 CONFIG.SYS

What is CONFIG.SYS? After the major DR DOS routines are loaded, DR DOS searches the root directory for a file called CONFIG.SYS. DR DOS then executes the commands which it finds in the CONFIG.SYS file.

The CONFIG.SYS file makes it possible for you to "tailor" your PC. For example, you can use this facility to set up your PC for extended keyboard functions or adding a RAM disk.

The CONFIG.SYS file may contain commands which specify various "set up" values for your PC. If there is no CONFIG.SYS file, or a specific command is omitted from the CONFIG.SYS file, then a default value is assumed.

The quickest way to create or edit the CONFIG.SYS file is to use the SETUP program:

SETUP Enter

Statements in the CONFIG.SYS file that begin with "?" contain commands that are optionally executed during system startup.

For example, a statement in the CONFIG.SYS file might read like this:

?"Should the line editing be turned on?" HISTORY = ON

Here the prompt "should the line editing be turned on?" is displayed. Then DR DOS waits for you to respond by pressing "Y" or "N". If you respond with "Y", the HISTORY = ON command is executed. If you respond with

"N" the HISTORY = ON command is not executed and DR DOS continues to process the next statement in the CONFIG.SYS file.

CONFIG.SYS Commands

You can see how your CONFIG.SYS file is set up by typing:

TYPE CONFIG.SYS [Enter]

The following screen should appear (your display may show different information):

```
SHELL=C:\COMMAND.COM C:\ /P /E:512
BREAK=ON
HIBUFFERS=15
FILES=20
FCBS=4,4
FASTOPEN=512
LASTDRIVE=E
HISTORY=ON, 256, OFF
COUNTRY=001,,C:\DRDOS\COUNTRY.SYS
HIDOS=ON
?"Load MemoryMAX software (Y/N)
"DEVICE=C:\DRDOS\EMM386.SYS /F=AUTO /K=3328
/B=FFFF /R=AUTO
DEVICE=C:\SSTORDRV.SYS
INSTALL=C:\DRDOS\LOGIN.EXE C:\DRDOS
```

Although you can edit the CONFIG.SYS directly with EDITOR, it's much easier to change it in the SETUP program.

SETUP [Enter]

Here's a summary of the commands that are used in the CONFIG.SYS file.

? You can confirm that you want to execute a specific command by placing a ? in front of the statement in the CONFIG.SYS file.

BREAK
DR DOS normally tests to see if [Ctrl]+[Pause] (also referred to as the <Break> key) was pressed during input or output to one of the standard I/O devices. You can also specify that [Ctrl]+[Pause] (or the <Break> key) is checked during disk operations.

If BREAK is ON, DR DOS looks to see if [Ctrl]+[Pause] was pressed whenever a DR DOS interrupt is called.

If the BREAK command is specified without parameters, the current status is displayed. The default status is OFF, unless previously changed by CONFIG.SYS or AUTOEXEC.BAT.

You should try and avoid forcefully interrupting a program and should only do it during programs that do not get "angry". If a program is processing files and the program is interrupted at a critical time, the files may not be closed correctly. This can result in the loss of data.

You can turn the break command on in CONFIG.SYS by typing:

```
Break = ON [Enter]
```

BUFFERS

Allow you to define the number of disk buffers (from 3 to 99). DR DOS reserves a certain number of buffers to transfer data between an application program and external storage device.

If there are not enough buffers available, the used buffers must be loaded with the actual data of the external storage device with every access. Since each buffer requires that 528 bytes of the work area be reserved (512 bytes for the buffer and 16 bytes for the management), the number of buffers affect the memory requirements.

The buffer size corresponds to the size of a sector on an external storage media. 30 buffers can be used on a 640K PC. We specify this with the BUFFERS command. This command is specified in the CONFIG.SYS. We can set up 30 data buffers with the following command:

```
BUFFERS = 30
```

Normally, by defining more buffers you can increase the speed of disk read and write operations. Some programs, such as dBASE III®, require that there be a minimum of 20 buffers:

```
BUFFERS = 20
```

185

CHAIN

When DR DOS first starts up, it automatically executes the commands in the file CONFIG.SYS. But you can specify an alternate configuration file with the CHAIN command. CHAIN tells DR DOS to transfer control to a different configuration file.

This lets you easily configure your computer for different applications. The CHAIN command is most often used with the "?" command, as in this example:

```
?"Execute CONFIG2?" CHAIN = C:\CONFIG2.SYS
```

This command lets you transfer to the CONFIG2.SYS file. If you answer by pressing Y, DR DOS switches to the alternate configuration file CONFIG2.SYS and the rest of the original configuration file is ignored.

Why would you use different configuration files? Let's say that one of your applications requires as much memory as possible to run. In this case you'd configure the system to maximize the amount of free RAM - eliminate memory resident programs, unnecessary device drivers, avoid RAM drives and so on. But another one of your applications is very disk intensive but does not require much memory. In this case you'd configure a large disk cache to minimize disk operations.

COUNTRY

Since DR DOS is used in different countries, which have different time and date formats, you can use the COUNTRY command to set the corresponding date and time format. The international telephone code of the desired country is used as the parameter.

DR DOS displays the date, currency symbol and decimal numbers in a country-related format. For example, the German notation for decimal numbers is different than the American notation. German notation uses the period to separate each series of three digits and uses the comma as a decimal point:

```
9.465.123,00
```

Select one code from the following country list:

Country		Country	
Australia	061	Japan	081
Belgium	032	Netherlands	031
Canada	002	Norway	047
Denmark	045	Spain	034
Finland	358	Sweden	046
France	033	Switzerland	041
Great Britain	044	United Kingdom	044
Israel	972	USA	001
Italy	039	West Germany	049

Use the ⬆ and ⬇ cursor keys to select the desired country. The selected country will appear darker and a blinking > symbol will appear next to the selected country. The following command sets the date and time specifications in West German format:

```
COUNTRY=049
```

DR DOS allows you to include the code page as the second parameter. The code page is a character set which redefines the country and keyboard information for non-US keyboards and systems. The following example is necessary for Germany:

```
COUNTRY=049,437
```

In addition, you have the option of giving the filename containing country-specific data. This is usually in the COUNTRY.SYS system diskette file:

```
COUNTRY=049,437,c:\DRDOS\COUNTRY.SYS
```

If no COUNTRY command is given in CONFIG.SYS, the default country number is 001 (USA), code page number 437 and the file \COUNTRY.SYS.

CPOS
Positions the cursor at a specified location on the screen.

DEVICE
Normally each device (such as a disk drive, system clock or keyboard) needs a device driver. The standard device drivers are automatically loaded by DR DOS.

187

You can also install device drivers that replace the standard input and output devices, or create a virtual disk (also known as a RAM disk).

A number of device drivers, such as ANSI.SYS (Screen device driver) and VDISK.SYS (Virtual disk drive device driver) are included with DR DOS. We'll explain each of these in Chapter 11.

DRIVPARM

Sets the drive parameters. This command lets you change the table of device parameters for a block device. The parameters for the command are:

/D:d	Logical disk drive specification where 0 represents logical drive A, 1 represents logical drive B and so on.
[/C]	The device's safety lever must be engaged.
[F:f]	Specifies the device type:
	0 360K
	1 1.2Mb drive
	2 720K drive
	7 1.44Mb drive
[H:h]	Number of read/write heads (1 or 2).
[/S:ss]	Number of sectors per track (1 to 63).
[/T:tt]	Number of tracks per side (40 or 80).

ECHO

You can display explanations during the system startup with the ECHO command. For example, the following command:

```
ECHO The VDISK is installed with 2Mb.
```

displays the specific information concerning VDISK on the screen.

EXIT   Terminates execution of CONFIG.SYS.

FASTOPEN

Allows you to create an internal buffer for file entries. When opening a file, DOS searches all necessary directories to locate the file. This can be time consuming if you're using a hard disk with several subdirectories. FASTOPEN stores the complete access path of the last used files. If one of these files is accessed again, it can be located very quickly from the information stored by the FASTOPEN command.

The following example reserves 100 entries in hard disk C:

```
FASTOPEN = C:100
```

FCBS

Defines maximum number of file control blocks which programs can open at the same time. A file control block retains information required by DOS for reading and writing to files.

The parameters for the command are:

m	Specifies the number of File Control Blocks that can be opened at one time (from 1 to 255).
n	Specifies the number of files that are protected from being closed if an attempt is made to open more than m files (from 1 to 255).

FILES

If a file on a diskette or hard drive is opened by an application program, DR DOS must build an area in memory to store information about that file, such as its filename, where it is found, if its access is limited, which data buffer should be used and in which relative position the next write or read access should be executed.

The area in which DR DOS keeps this information is reserved with the FILES command:

```
FILES = 30
```

Defines the maximum number of open files (from 20 to 255). The default is 20.

GOSUB

Jumps to a label during execution, executes the commands following the label, then jumps back when a RETURN statement is encountered.

GOTO
>   Jumps to a label.

HIBUFFERS
>   Sets the number of disk buffers and attempts to allocate them in high memory.

HIDEVICE
>   Identical to DEVICE but HIDEVICE loads extra device drivers (ANSI.SYS, CACHE.EXE and VDISK.SYS) into upper memory. We'll discuss these device drivers in Chapter 11.

HIDOS
>   Loads the DR DOS operating system kernal into upper memory.

HIINSTALL
>   Identical to INSTALL but HIINSTALL loads the specified program (CURSOR.EXE, KEYB.EXE, CHARE.EXE and others) into upper memory.

>   For example:

```
HIINSTALL = C:\DRDOS\KEYB.COM GR
```

HISTORY
>   Turns on the line editing of DR DOS commands. We discussed HISTORY in Section 1.2.

>   The DR DOS command line editor can perform expanded editing functions if HISTORY = ON. When activated the commands are saved in a buffer sequentially. You can then use the keyboard to recall and edit previous commands that were saved in the buffer.

>   Type the following line to activate the command:

```
HISTORY = ON
```

>   You can specify how large the buffer should be (between 128 and 4096 bytes) and if the editor should be in the insert mode by default.

```
HISTORY = ON, 1024, OFF
```

This line turns HISTORY on, allocates a buffer size of 1024 bytes and turns the insert mode off.

INSTALL

Loads a program during the system start. These include the following programs:

>
> CURSOR.EXE
>
> GRAFTABL.COM
>
> GRAPHICS.COM
>
> KEYB.COM
>
> NLSFUNC.EXE
>
> PRINT.EXE
>
> SHARE.EXE

Type the following to install the program (we're installing KEYB.COM in this example):

```
INSTALL = C:\DRDOS\KEYB.COM UK [Enter]
```

LASTDRIVE

Allows you to set the maximum number of useable drives and to specify the last drive letter.

Since external storage devices are addressed using the device drivers or different configurations can be arranged for internal devices so they can be used like independent disk drives, it's necessary to limit the number of drives DR DOS can handle.

The default value is 5 for LASTDRIVE. This corresponds to drives A through E. The drive identifier of the last desired drive is used as the parameter for this command. You should note that you must build a data structure for each drive specified. This requires room in the memory. You should use only as many drives as absolutely necessary. For example, if you want 7 drive labels, insert the following command in the CONFIG.SYS file:

```
LASTDRIVE = G
```

REM You can insert comments in the configuration file by using the REM command:

```
REM 4Mb expanded memory has been installed.
```

No action is performed by the REM command.

RETURN

Directs the operating system to jump back after executing a GOSUB or SWITCH command.

SET   Defines the environmental variables.

SHELL

Normally when DR DOS is booted, the COMMAND.COM command processor is loaded and started. It recognizes the DR DOS commands. However, you can substitute a replacement command interpreter by using the SHELL command.

The SHELL command lets you specify the name and path of the interpreter and the amount of environment space (memory) that should be set aside. For example, you can add the following line to your CONFIG.SYS:

```
SHELL = C:\COM\COMMAND.COM C:\COM /P/E:1024
```

This line tells DR DOS to load the file C:\COM\COMMAND as the command interpreter when booting. DR DOS searches in the C:\COM subdirectory when the transient section of the command line interpreter needs to be loaded. The /P parameter tells DR DOS to load COMMAND.COM permanently in memory and the /E:1024 parameter sets the size of the system environment to 1024 bytes.

If your computer does not use a hard drive, you can install a small RAM disk. Copy COMMAND.COM to this RAM disk and tell DR DOS to look for COMMAND.COM on the RAM disk with the SHELL command.

SWITCH

Permits switching between different configuration routines within the same CONFIG.SYS file.

TIMEOUT

Forces the system to ignore a ? or SWITCH command if the prompt is not answered within a specified period of time.

11.2 The PATH Command

The PATH command is an important tool when working with directories and subdirectories. For example, suppose the file you need is called NEWINFO, however the current directory is C:\GARY\PRIVATE and NEWINFO is located in a directory named INFO. You won't be able to access NEWINFO from the PRIVATE directory. DR DOS would respond with:

```
Command or filename not recognized
```

However, by using the PATH command, DR DOS will search in all named directories but does not change the current directory. It tells DOS where to look for any DOS commands and programs. For example, if you entered:

```
PATH  C:\DRDOS;C:\PCTOOLS;C:\123;  [Enter]
```

The PATH command specifies which directories that DR DOS is to search for to find executable commands. You must separate each directory by a semicolon.

When you type a command at the DR DOS command prompt, DR DOS searches the current directory for the command. If it isn't found, then DR DOS searches the C:\DRDOS directory, then the C:\PCTOOLS directory and finally the C:\123 directory.

If the command file is not in any of those directories, the following message will appear:

```
Command or filename not recognized
```

You can include the PATH command in the AUTOEXEC.BAT so that DR DOS would automatically look in drive C: (or whatever drive) for DOS commands.

Cancel PATH by typing:

```
PATH ;[Enter]
```

11.3 The APPEND Command

Setting Paths   The PATH command is used to specify the directories to find executable files (files with .COM, .EXE or .BAT files). The APPEND command is used to specify the directories to find other files.

When an application is searching for a file, it will first search the current directory. If the APPEND command is used, then the directories specified in the command are searched to find the file.

Example:

```
APPEND C:\HELP
```

This command sets a directory search path to C:\HELP. If an application is searching for a file and cannot find it in the current directory, it then searches for the file in the C:\HELP directory.

APPEND is an external DR DOS command (PATH is internal). Therefore it's active only when you call (load) it.

On the first call you can use the /X:ON switch or /X:OFF switch (default). APPEND then uses the defined paths for searching for the program files (extensions .BAT, .EXE and .COM).

Also, on the first call, you can use the /E:ON switch or /E:OFF (default) to store the search path in the environment.

The other switches available for APPEND are the /PATH:ON (default) and /PATH:OFF. They represent the path in which you want to search for files. You can define multiple paths but separate each by semicolons.

Cancel APPEND by typing:

```
APPEND ;Enter
```

Two final notes on using APPEND:

1.   When a file within the defined search path is found and is opened for reading, some applications may open a NEW file in the standard directory - the old file remains unchanged.

2.   Cancel the APPEND search string before using the BACKUP command.

11.4 The Keyboard Layout

The keyboard layout for the different international keyboards is specified by the KEYB command. When you use KEYB, a keyboard program displays the characters corresponding to the keyboard layout.

The U.S. keyboard layout is selected by default. To change to another country, type the following command:

```
KEYB <country_code> (Enter)
```

Use the following table to select the <country_code>:

Country	Abbr	Country code
Belgium	BE	437 850
Canada (French)	CF	863 850
Denmark	DK	865 850
Finland	SU	437 850
France	FR	437 850
Germany	GR	437 850
Italy	IT	437 850
Latin America	LA	437 850
Netherlands	NL	437 850
Norway	NO	865 850
Portugal	PO	869 850
Spain	SP	437 850
Sweden	SV	437 850
Swiss (French)	SF	437 850
Swiss (German)	SG	437 850
United Kingdom	UK	437 850
United States	US	437 850

11.5 The Environment Area

The DR DOS system environment area is an area of memory that is used as a communication area for named variables. Different applications can store and/or retrieve values from the environment area.

SET Command The SET command allows you to define or display an environment variable name and value.

The following is an example of its syntax:

```
SET variable=value
```

Variable refers to the name of the variable. All characters in the name are converted by DR DOS to uppercase characters. The value refers to the string of characters that specifies the current value of <variable>.

If you omit both variable and value, all of the current environment variable names and values are displayed. If value is omitted, variable and its value are deleted from the environment. Type the following:

```
SET [Enter]
```

Will display information similar to the following:

```
COMSPEC=C:\COMMAND.COM
OS=DRDOS
VER=6.0
PATH=C:\DRDOS
PROMPT=[DR DOS] $P$G
```

The following example:

```
SET CLIPPER = F050
```

creates a named variable called CLIPPER. This variable is set to a value of FO50. An application can inspect the environment area if it wants to determine if this named variable was previously set.

Another example is one of the environment variables called COMSPEC. It contains the path used to reload COMMAND.COM. Other programs can then reference COMSPEC as necessary.

Two other standard environment names are PATH and PROMPT (not to be confused with the DR DOS commands of the same name). These names can be displayed and modified with the SET command or the PATH and PROMPT commands.

USER Variable   The following command informs a program that the user is named Smith (provided the program reads the environment variable USER):

```
SET USER=Smith
```

The following command deletes the variable USER:

```
SET USER=
```

You can confirm the above examples by typing:

```
SET  (Enter)
```

after each example.

The following command tells DOS that COMMAND.COM is located in a different location:

```
SET comspec=C:\DOS\COMMAND.COM
```

Note: If you load a new command processor and then modify the environment, the changes made will not be preserved after the EXIT command. The environment of the calling command processor will be restored.

11.6 The System Prompt

*PROMPT
Command*

When waiting for you to enter a command, DR DOS displays the system prompt. You can change the appearance of the system prompt by using the PROMPT command. For example, to display the drive identifier and the current path, use this command:

```
PROMPT $p$g
```

You can include the appropriate command in your AUTOEXEC.BAT file. The <string> parameter is composed of printable characters or the following codes (refer to the table below). These codes can be used anywhere in the string and as often as necessary:

```
PROMPT <string>
```

The characters you use for a new system prompt are listed in Column B of the following table. Type the PROMPT command followed by the dollar sign ($) and then the character from Column A:

A	B
$	$ character
t	current time
d	current date
p	current path
v	DR DOS version number
n	current drive
g	> character
l	< character
b	I character
q	= character
h	backspace character
e	Esc character
x	Execute a command on return to the system prompt. Specify the file with a SET expression to set a value for PEXEC.
_	CR LF characters

DR DOS ignores a character pair in the prompt string if the dollar sign is followed by a character not found in the above table.

For example, use the following PROMPT command to display the date and time in the prompt (omitting the year) and the current drive and directory:

```
PROMPT $d$h$h$h$h$h, $t$h$h$h$_$p$g Enter
```

If DR DOS responds with either of the following error messages:

```
Not enough environment memory!
Filename too long
```

You must shorten the PROMPT command or delete unnecessary SET symbols.

11.7 Device Drivers

Device drivers are programs which enable DR DOS to communicate with external devices such as the keyboard, screen, printer and other peripherals.

The concept of the device driver is very flexible and makes the development of many additional devices for your computer possible. This open architecture is certainly a reason for the wide spread use of the personal computer today. DR DOS offers a defined interface in the device drivers. The construction and control of the device drivers has been determined exactly and documented so that device drivers exist for many different applications.

*Types of
Device Drivers*
There are several device drivers supplied by DR DOS. These include ANSI.SYS, DISPLAY.SYS, DRIVER.SYS HIDOS.SYS, PRINTER.SYS, VDISK.SYS and others.

We discussed EMM386.SYS and EMMXMA.SYS in Chapter 9 (Memory Management).

Some of the device drivers supplied with DR DOS are installed at the start of the system. These drivers are CON, PRN, LPT1, COM1 and others. These device drivers are overwritten when a device driver with the same name is loaded from CONFIG.SYS.

When installing DR DOS you are asked if you want to load the EMM386.SYS, PC-Kwik (the disk cache) and VDISK.SYS drivers. You can also choose to load these drivers later using the SETUP program. A third way to load these unit drivers is to enter them directly in the CONFIG.SYS. This assumes that you have some experience in operating computers. We recommend you use SETUP. Study the SETUP program and then change some of the parameters if you are looking to make some improvements. For more information, refer to the SETUP program in Chapter 1.

ANSI.SYS

Using
ANSI.SYS

The most frequently used device driver is ANSI.SYS. This is a programmable file which supports the keyboard and the screen.

ANSI.SYS is frequently used because it provides the additional options that many applications and programs require for screen control, cursor control or keyboard control.

The information contained in the ANSI.SYS follows the recommendations of the American National Standards Institute (ANSI). Therefore, you can use it to define individual keys and it can evaluate the ANSI escape sequence (all starting at 1B hex) for screen control.

You should load the ANSI.SYS driver from your CONFIG.SYS program. When ANSI.SYS is in the CONFIG.SYS, DR DOS will automatically load it at startup. To do this, first load the EDITOR program by typing:

```
EDITOR CONFIG.SYS (Enter)
```

This will call the Editor program and load the CONFIG.SYS file. Then type the following command:

```
DEVICE = C:\DRDOS\ANSI.SYS
```

You can also use the SETUP or INSTALL programs to include the ANSI.SYS driver.

Changing
Keyboard
Layouts

After ANSI.SYS is loaded, you can switch the keyboard/screen display between the US keyboard layout and the layout specified with the KEYB command using (Ctrl)+(Alt)+(F1) for the US layout and (Ctrl)+(Alt)+(F2) for the other specified layout.

The following is the list of escape sequences available when ANSI.SYS is installed. Parameters are printed in *italics*:

ESC [2 J   Clear the screen.

ESC [K   Clear to end of line.
                  Erases the remainder of a line (from the cursor position
                  to the end of the line).

ESC [$x;y$ H   Define the cursor position.

ESC [$x;y$ f   Positions the cursor in column x, line y.
                  If one or both of the parameters are omitted, the default
                  is 1.

ESC [y A   Move cursor up.
                  Moves the cursor up x lines. If the x parameter is
                  omitted, the cursor is moved one line. The column
                  remains unchanged. The cursor cannot be moved past
                  the top of the screen.

ESC [y B   Move cursor down.
                  Moves the cursor down y lines. If the y parameter is
                  omitted, the cursor is moved one line. The column
                  remains unchanged. The cursor cannot be moved past
                  the bottom of the screen.

ESC [x C   Move cursor right.
                  Moves the cursor x characters to the right. If the x
                  parameter is omitted, the cursor is moved one character.
                  The line remains unchanged. If the cursor is located in
                  the rightmost column, the command has no effect.

ESC [x D   Move cursor left.
                  Moves the cursor x characters to the left. If the x
                  parameter is omitted, the cursor is moved one character.
                  The line remains unchanged. If the cursor is located in
                  the leftmost column, the command has no effect.

ESC [s   Save current cursor position.

ESC [u   Send cursor to saved position.

ESC [6n   Send cursor position control (see next command).

ESC [y,x R   Set standard cursor position.
                  The cursor position defined here is automatically used
                  when the control sequence $6n$ is specified.

ESC [=n h 1 or Set screen mode.
ESC [=h 1 or   These values set the screen mode. The parameter n can
ESC [=n h   have the following values:

0	40x25 monochrome
1	40x25 color
2	80x25 monochrome
3	80x25 color
4	320x200 color
5	320x200 monochrome
6	640x200 monochrome
7	Word wrap

ESC [n ;...n m Set screen attribute.
The following codes set attributes in text mode on
certain video controller cards:

0	None
1	Bold
2	Normal
3	Italic
5	Blinking
6	Fast blinking
7	Reverse video
8	Invisible
30	Black foreground
31	Red foreground
32	Green foreground
33	Yellow foreground
34	Blue foreground
35	Magenta foreground
36	Cyan foreground
37	White foreground
40	Black background
41	Red background
42	Green background
43	Yellow background
44	Blue background
45	Magenta background
46	Cyan background
47	White background
48	Superscript
49	Subscript

ESC [n ; n ;...n p
> Assign string y+...+z to key x.
> Allows you to assign string variables to a specific key. For example, you could assign the most important DOS commands to their starting letters plus the (Alt) key. The string must be enclosed in quotes, or you can define the ASCII code or a single character in decimal. The parameters are separated by semicolons.

You can define more than one key in a single escape sequence by repeating Esc-[. A semicolon (;) <u>cannot</u> precede the terminating **p**.

VDISK.SYS

Installing a RAM Disk

If you have a PC with only one floppy disk drive, you've probably discovered that you had to change ("swap") diskettes frequently while working with most programs or applications. This includes external DR DOS commands such as FORMAT and DISKCOPY.

A program on the DOS system disk allocates a certain amount of memory in the computer to act as a RAM disk. You can read data from this RAM disk, write to it, copy to and copy from it. Its main disadvantage is that it's only temporary. Once you switch off your PC, data stored on the RAM disk is gone unless you copied that data to a disk before turning off the computer.

This RAM disk is called VDISK.SYS under DR DOS. The following is an example of the syntax of VDISK.SYS:

```
DEVICE=C:\DRDOS\VDISK.SYS [<size>][<sectors>] [<files>]
    [/e:sectors] [/x]
```

Here size represents the number of kilobytes to be reserved for the RAM disk. This value can range from 1 to 256K or extended memory. The default is 64K. At least 64K of memory must be left available for applications.

The sectors are the size of the virtual sector. Use either 128, 256 or 512 bytes.

The dir is the number of virtual directory entries (from 2 to 512). The default is 64.

The /e option is used only on IBM PC ATs with extended memory. It specifies that the virtual disk is located in this extended memory area above the 1Mb boundary. The default is 8.

The /x option locates the RAM disk in expanded memory and can be defined as up to 32Mb.

The following example defines a RAM disk with a capacity of 150K. Each sector is 256 bytes long and 100 directory entries are allowed:

```
DEVICE=VDISK.SYS 150 256 100
```

12. Batch Files

12. Batch Files

Normally DR DOS commands are entered from the keyboard following the system prompt (for example, C>). After you press (Enter), DR DOS immediately analyzes the command and then executes it.

Sometimes it's convenient to combine frequently used command sequences into a batch. A file of commands is called a batch file.

Specific
Extensions

You can easily recognize a batch file by their .BAT extension. This extension not only informs users about the file, but informs the computer as well. Therefore, never use this extension for any other type of file.

You can use any eight characters for a batch filename but it must use .BAT for an extension.

Execute a batch file from the system prompt simply by typing its filename (without the .BAT extension) and pressing the (Enter) key. The commands are then executed in the order they appear within the batch file itself.

Using batch files can save you time and effort. To prove this, we'll provide a simple example.

There are three methods to create a batch file: Your word processor, the EDITOR, or the COPY CON command.

As you've already noticed, certain commands in DR DOS can require a lot of typing. These same commands can be written into a batch file that has a short, easy to remember name. Let's assume you frequently use the command DIR I SORT to sort the directory. You can create a small batch file using EDITOR to do this for you. Type the following:

```
EDITOR dirsort.bat (Enter)
```

When prompted whether you want to create a new file, press (Y):

When the EDITOR screen appears, type the commands in the order you want them executed. Type the following lines, making certain to press (Enter) after each line:

```
CD\DRDOS [Enter]
ECHO OFF [Enter]
CLS [Enter]
DIR | SORT [Enter]
```

When you have entered the batch file, press [Ctrl]+[K] [X] to save the file and to exit EDITOR.

At the system prompt type the following:

```
DIRSORT [Enter]
```

The batch file sorts and displays the sorted DRDOS directory.

Now, let's create a batch file that automatically formats a disk and includes the necessary data used for booting. This gives us a universal program that will make disks for our own applications (e.g., word processors, databases, etc.).

We could type these commands in one by one, but why bother? Writing a batch file saves time and effort, and saves our typing in the commands later. Make sure you're in the root directory of drive C: and enter the following batch file, named INSF.BAT (INStant Format):

```
CD\DRDOS [Enter]
FORMAT A:/S
ECHO OFF [Enter]
CLS [Enter]
```

Use caution when adding commands such as FORMAT to a batch file, or you may accidentally format a disk you didn't want formatted.

A note on using variables

You can pass up to nine variables (separated by spaces) to a batch file. DR DOS names these variables %1 through %12. The %0 represents the name of the command itself. You can use the variables as often as you like in the batch file.

To enter a percent sign (%) in a batch file, use a double percent sign (%%). We do not recommend using the characters <, >, or | as text characters in filenames.

12.1 Batch File Commands

In addition to normal DR DOS commands, there are several commands that can be used only in batch files. Here's an overview of batch file commands:

:LABEL   Allows you to define a label for the GOTO command (see GOTO in this section). DR DOS recognizes the first eight characters only, so make certain not to use the same eight characters for different labels.

@   Prevents DR DOS from displaying the command when the batch file is executed.

CALL   Allows you to load and execute another batch file within a batch job. When the batch file finishes running, the system returns to the original batch file.

ECHO   Allows you to display text or a string on the screen. Also allows you to change the echo status.

ON   Displays all commands within the batch file.

OFF   The commands within the batch file are <u>not</u> displayed.

If all variables are omitted, the current status of ECHO is displayed. You can display messages during the execution of a batch file.

FOR   Allows you to repeat a command in a batch file for a series of filenames:

```
FOR %%<var> in (<list>) DO <command>
```

%%<var> is a variable to be assigned a value within the series of filenames. The filenames must be separated by spaces. The value of %%<var> represents one of the filenames, according to the order that the filename appears in <list>. FOR does accept wildcards.

You can use any DR DOS command for <command> but you cannot use another FOR command.

GOTO   Allows you to branch to a label in a batch program. A label is a character string. Only the first eight characters are significant and therefore must be different from other labels.

211

In a batch file, <label> is preceded by a colon (:). The following is an example of an infinite loop:

```
ECHO OFF
:START
TYPE SAMPLE.TXT
GOTO START
```

This batch file can be terminated only by pressing [Ctrl]+[Pause] (also called <Break>). After you press this key combination, the following message (or one similar) appears:

```
Halt Batch Process (Y/N)?
```

Press [Y] to terminate the batch file or press [N] to continue the batch file.

IF   Allows you to test a condition and execute the corresponding DR DOS command. IF tests the condition and executes the DR DOS command if the test is true (false if NOT is specified).

The condition is one of the following three types of tests performed by DR DOS:

EXIST<filename>	True if <filename> exists
<string1> == <string2>	Strings 1 and 2 must be identical
ERRORLEVEL<number>	True if errorlevel (exit code) is greater than or equal to <number>

The ERRORLEVEL is a system variable that is usually set by applications or other DOS commands. This allows you, for example, to test the return codes from the BACKUP command. You must test the values in descending order because IF tests for a condition greater than or equal to the specified value:

PAUSE   Allows you to temporarily halt the execution of a batch file and display a message. Execution of the batch file resumes when you press any key (except [Ctrl]+[Pause] or <Break>).

REM   Allows you to insert a comment in a batch file.

REM displays the comment if ECHO is ON. However, the comment is not displayed if ECHO is OFF.

SHIFT   Allows you to shift the list of variables one position to the left. You're limited to 10 variables (%0 through %9) in a batch file.

The following batch file displays the contents of all the variables passed to it, however many variables are present:

```
ECHO OFF
:LOOP
IF "%1" == "" GOTO DONE
ECHO %1
SHIFT
GOTO LOOP
:DONE
ECHO DONE!
```

SHIFT sidesteps this limitation by shifting the variable list to the left. By doing this, the contents of %0 are replaced by the contents of %1, the contents of %1 are replaced by %2, etc. The previous contents of %0 are lost.

12.2   Modifying AUTOEXEC.BAT

In this section we'll discuss a specific type of batch file called AUTOEXEC.BAT. This type of batch file is found on almost all "bootable" disks. The only thing that is different about AUTOEXEC.BAT from other batch files is its very specific name.

As its name indicates (AUTOEXECute), the AUTOEXEC.BAT file will self-start. This will occur immediately after the disk has booted or after the operating system is loaded from the disk.

There are several advantages of using an AUTOEXEC.BAT file:

1. You do not need to enter commands through the keyboard in order for them to execute. However, in order to use this batch file, the disk must be formatted with the system.

2. Once the computer is started, the AUTOEXEC.BAT file allows you to "steer" the PC in any direction.

Now we must write an AUTOEXEC.BAT file that will execute the CHKDSK command.

Load the AUTOEXEC.BAT in the EDITOR:

```
EDITOR AUTOEXEC.BAT Enter
```

Then add the commands you would like to execute when the computer starts. For example, the following AUTOEXEC.BAT example will display the date, time, CHKDSK and will sort the directory before you type in anything from the keyboard (except for DATE and TIME):

```
@ECHO OFF
:DRDOSBEG
PATH C:\DRDOS
VERIFY OFF
PROMPT $P$G
DATE
TIME
CHKDSK
DIR | SORT
MEMMAX -U >NUL
:DRDOSEND
```

Labels   Note these two labels in the previous listing:

```
:DRDOSBEG
:DRDOSEND
```

SETUP processes all DR DOS commands and data between these labels. If you want to include statements from other operating systems (e.g., UNIX), place these statements outside of the labels.

The PATH command tells DR DOS where to look for the command, program and batch files.

Other statements you can include in the AUTOEXEC.BAT file are TIME and DATE, SET and PATH.

Perform a warm start (press [Ctrl]+[Alt]+[Del]) to test whether this batch file works.

AUTOEXEC   As soon as the operating system is loaded, the computer will execute the AUTOEXEC.BAT file. The computer will send a message to the screen telling you that the CHKDSK command is being loaded from the disk.

On the screen, you'll see the results of the CHKDSK command followed by the results of the DIR command.

13. Error Messages

13. Error Messages

You've seen so far that your PC is a useful tool which provides you with many capabilities. However, a PC is also very demanding. Remember that your PC responds only to what it understands. This means that it does what it's told, if possible, and not what you want it to do.

As humans, we make mistakes. Most people suffer some stress when they find themselves learning about any computer for the first time. In the heat of this stress, the beginning user can make some errors that he or she may not know how to fix, or if the errors can be fixed at all. Other errors can be caused by typing errors.

If you get an error, don't panic. Both beginning and expert users alike make mistakes and invoke errors. Keep this in mind, and stay calm as you try to figure out what went wrong.

The first section of this chapter lists some of the most common errors in DR DOS and how you can correct these errors as they happen. In the second section, we describe the situations when errors are likely to occur.

13.1 DR DOS Error Messages

The following is an alphabetical list of the most important error messages. This listing also tells you what types of errors could have caused each of these messages and how you should react to them.

Bad media type
> The diskette in the floppy disk drive is bad or not formatted correctly. Try to reformat this diskette or use another diskette.

Bad or missing file
> DR DOS failed to locate the CONFIG.SYS file. You should modify your CONFIG.SYS so that DR DOS is able to read it.

BOOT error
> Something went wrong when the operating system was loading. Switch off your PC and then switch it on again. If the same message appears, repeat the procedure and place your DOS disk in drive A:.

Command or filename not recognized
You've either made a typing mistake while entering a command or that particular file (external command) does not exist on the disk. Check your spelling and/or the disk directory.

Data Error
This indicates an error when you were accessing a specified device. Make certain the device is properly connected. This indicates a more serious error if it occurs on the hard disk. Backup all non-corrupt files, then use CHKDSK or format the hard disk.

Destination disk is full
The destination disk is full or doesn't have sufficient space to save the file you're trying to copy. Insert another formatted disk in the drive and repeat the procedure. If this isn't possible, then erase unnecessary files from the destination disk.

Drive not ready
You may not have placed a diskette in the drive or closed the drive door. It's also possible that you tried to save a file on a disk that is write-protected. Press the Ⓐ key (Abort) to exit the entire operation.

File already exists or file not found
While using the RENAME command, either you've specified a name that already exists in the particular directory or the source file could not be found. Check the directory to verify the source filename and check whether a file already exists with the new name.

File not found
This message will appear when DR DOS cannot find a filename which you called with a DR DOS command. You should look at the directory on the specified disk to see if the file is actually on the disk.

Halt Batch Process (Y/N)
You've interrupted the execution of a batch file by pressing Ⓒtrl+Ⓟause. Press Ⓝ to continue executing the batch file or press Ⓨ to stop the batch file and return to the system prompt.

Invalid date specified
You've made a mistake while using the DATE command.

Invalid file name
You may have incorrectly typed the filename. Retype the correct filename.

Invalid file specification
You may have typed the correct filename but the wrong path. Retype the correct path and filename.

Invalid number of parameters
> You added too many or incorrect parameters (switches) following a command.

Invalid parameter
> The parameter you typed following a command is not recognized by DR DOS.

Invalid time specified
> You've made a mistake while using the TIME command.

Label <name> not found
> You included a GOTO statement in a batch file which refers to a nonexistent label. Make the necessary changes in the batch file.

Not enough memory...
> Your PC doesn't have enough memory available to perform the task. Try to free some memory by removing memory resident programs.

Not ready error
> The disk drive or other device you're trying to access doesn't respond. Make certain the diskette is properly inserted and the drive is closed.

Path not found
> You typed an incorrect path.

Parameter not recognized
> The command was entered incorrectly. Please check your parameters.

Sector not found...
> DR DOS detected an error on a disk. Make certain the diskette is formatted correctly. If you still receive this error message, repeat the procedure with another formatted diskette.

Source and Destination cannot be the same file
> You cannot place two files with the same name in the same directory.

13.2 Error Situations

The error numbers we're using in this section do not correspond to any DR DOS standards. We chose this numbering because we felt that these were among the "top ten" errors that occur.

Error 1 Many problems occur when your boot your system. Some very inexpensive PC systems don't include operating system disks with the package and make you purchase DOS separately.

After you switch on the PC, the messages we described earlier do not appear on the screen. Instead, another message, similar to this one, appears:

```
System files not found
```

Check the following for potential error sources:

1. Did you insert the proper system diskette(s) in the disk drives?

2. Did you close the disk drive lever (5-1/4" format) or press the disk into the drive until it locked into place (3-1/2" format)?

3. DR DOS may be on the hard disk. Switch on the computer again but make certain that a diskette is in any floppy disk drive.

Error 2 You want to execute a command but your PC returns the following or a similar message:

```
Not ready error reading drive A
Abort, Retry, Fail?
```

This means that DR DOS cannot read the disk in drive A:. Check for the following as potential error sources:

1. The diskette may not be formatted correctly. Press the Ⓐ key to abort. Enter a DIR command, or even a VOL command to check for a directory or a volume name. If the disk was not formatted, it will repeat the message. Press the Ⓐ key to abort. Remove the disk and insert a copy of the DOS disk. Enter:

    ```
    FORMAT A:Enter
    ```

    Follow the instructions for formatting the disk.

2. Another possibility to check: Is the disk drive lever closed and is the disk firmly in place (depending on your disk format)? Make sure and press the [R] key to retry.

Error 3   You enter a DR DOS command but your PC doesn't react.

Check the following for potential error sources:

1. Did you press the [Enter] key after entering the command? In most cases, you must press this key before the PC executes a DR DOS command.

2. You may have accidentally pressed [Shift] or [Backspace] instead of the [Enter] key.

3. If neither of these are the cause, press the [Ctrl]+[Alt] and [Del] key combination to perform a warm start. Then try entering a command when the system prompt appears (remember to press [Enter] at the end of the command).

Error 4   You enter a command as it appears in this book. Your PC displays the following or a similar message:

```
Command or filename not recognized
```

Check the following for potential error sources:

1. You may have incorrectly typed the command. Compare it with the word as it appears in this book or with the program name as listed in the disk directory. If you type the directory command for drive A:, make sure it reads:

```
DIR A:
```

and not:

```
DIRA:
```

2. If you insert a disk that doesn't contain an external DR DOS command, your PC will attempt to load the command from disk. The previous error message appears if the PC cannot locate the command. Remove the disk currently in drive A:. Insert a DR DOS disk in drive A:. Make sure the system prompt reads A>. Try the command again.

3. If the command is not a DR DOS command, then it must be a program name. Check the following:

- Is the disk containing the program in the proper drive? Check the drive specifier (look at the system prompt).
- Are you in the correct directory or subdirectory path for access? Check the directory by displaying it with CD.

4. Check your version of DR DOS using the VER command. Some commands may only be available on newer versions of DR DOS.

Error 5   You enter FORMAT A: by mistake and DR DOS prompts you to insert the diskette in drive A:. However, you realize that this is the wrong diskette. Remove the disk from drive A: and press the Ⓒⓣⓡⓛ+Ⓒ combination. This key combination terminates the FORMAT command.

Error 6   You have two drives and have created several subdirectories. After copying a file from drive A: to drive C:, now you can't find it. Your PC has probably copied the file to a completely different directory.

Check the following for potential error sources:

1. You probably selected a subdirectory as a current directory and wanted to copy into the root directory. Remember that using the following command doesn't guarantee that the PC will read from or write to the root directory of either disk:

   ```
   COPY A:FILENAME B:
   ```

   To copy from one root directory to the other root directory, use backslashes to return to the root directory:

   ```
   COPY A:\FILENAME B:\
   ```

2. Test which directories are active on each drive. You can do this using one of two commands:

   ```
   CD
   PROMPT $P
   ```

   The PC will then display the valid directory for the current drive. If you enter the drive specifier (for example, A:), DR DOS accepts this as the valid directory for this drive.

Appendices

A. DR DOS vs. MS-DOS

You may wonder, why invest in a new PC operating system when there are thousands of programs and applications already available to work with MS-DOS.

Although DR DOS is an emulation of MS-DOS, it includes several extra features. If you're familiar with MS-DOS you'll appreciate the differences which DR DOS offers.

The following tables show the differences between DR DOS and MS-DOS. They include a short description of the DR DOS feature and the location in this book where you'll find additional information:

Advanced Memory Management

DR DOS 6.0	YES	
MS-DOS 3.30		NO
MS-DOS 4.01		NO
MS-DOS 5.0	YES	

DR DOS 6.0 includes device drivers which allow you to quickly move the operating system kernal of DR DOS into higher or upper memory. This allows you to free this memory for other applications.

DR DOS also supports using upper memory (between 640K and 1Mb) for loading device drivers, TSR (Terminate and Stay Resident) programs and networking software.

See Chapter 10.

Cursor size and blink rate control

DR DOS 6.0	YES	
MS-DOS 3.30		NO
MS-DOS 4.01		NO
MS-DOS 5.0		NO

The CURSOR command permits control of the cursor's appearance and blink rate.

Disk caching

DR DOS 6.0	YES	
MS-DOS 3.30		NO
MS-DOS 4.01	YES	
MS-DOS 5.0	YES	

This disk utility can use base, expanded or extended memory to buffer disk reads. You can access it from the command line:

CACHE [Enter]

Or use the SETUP program.

Easy-Menu Driven Installation

DR DOS 6.0	YES	
MS-DOS 3.30		NO
MS-DOS 4.01		NO
MS-DOS 5.0		NO

INSTALL allows you to install a small, medium or large DR DOS system. INSTALL includes context-sensitive help screens. You can cancel the INSTALL program at any time by pressing the [F10] key.

See Chapter 1.

Executes from ROM

DR DOS 6.0	YES	
MS-DOS 3.30		NO
MS-DOS 4.01		NO
MS-DOS 5.0		NO

Several manufacturers include DR DOS in ROM. This is useful in laptop and notebook computers. For example, Award Software has a ROM-executable version of DR DOS available. Cardinal Technologies has released a DOS ROM which allows any computer to boot from ROM.

File Compression

DR DOS 6.0	YES	
MS-DOS 3.30		NO
MS-DOS 4.01		NO
MS-DOS 5.0		NO

DR DOS features DiskMAX, disk utilities for caching and file compression.

File Transfer Utility Is Standard

DR DOS 6.0	YES	
MS-DOS 3.30		NO
MS-DOS 4.01		NO
MS-DOS 5.0		NO

Do you need to transfer files from a laptop to a desktop PC? No problem because DR DOS includes the FILELINK utility. It allows you to transfer files over a serial cable (at a rate up to 155,200 baud) from one computer to another without the need of a modem.

Full DOS applications support

DR DOS 6.0	YES	
MS-DOS 3.30	YES	
MS-DOS 4.01	YES	
MS-DOS 5.0	YES	

Full-screen text editor

DR DOS 6.0	YES	
MS-DOS 3.30		NO
MS-DOS 4.01		NO
MS-DOS 5.0	YES	

DR DOS includes the EDITOR program to replace the EDLIN single line editor in MS-DOS versions prior to MS-DOS 5.0. MS-DOS 5.0 includes EDIT, a full-screen editor program.

EDITOR supports block editing functions. These functions allow you to move, copy and delete entire blocks of text. You can even write a block of text to another file or incorporate a block text from another file.

Graphic User Interface (ViewMAX)

DR DOS 6.0	YES	
MS-DOS 3.30		NO
MS-DOS 4.01	YES	
MS-DOS 5.0	YES	

ViewMAX is excellent if you've become familiar working with icons and folders or if you're tired of typing commands. You can use either the keyboard or a mouse in ViewMAX.

Hard disk partitions greater than 32Mb

DR DOS 6.0	YES	
MS-DOS 3.30		NO
MS-DOS 4.01	YES	
MS-DOS 5.0	YES	

If you find that disk partitions of 32Mb under MS-DOS is too limiting, DR DOS supports hard disk partitioning up to a maximum of 512Mb per partition.

Help Screens Built-in

DR DOS 6.0	YES	
MS-DOS 3.30		NO
MS-DOS 4.01		NO
MS-DOS 5.0	YES	

If you need more information on external DR DOS commands, all you need to do is type the command followed by /H or /?:

APPEND/H (Enter)

Then DR DOS displays a syntax of the command and a list of valid options or parameters you can use.

LIM/EMS 4.0 Supported

DR DOS 6.0	YES	
MS-DOS 3.30		NO
MS-DOS 4.01	YES	
MS-DOS 5.0	YES	

DR DOS supports the LIM/EMS 4.0 for all 80x86 processors and on IBM Expanded Adapters (XMA) or compatible memory boards.

Multiple Command Line Recall

DR DOS 6.0	YES	
MS-DOS 3.30		NO
MS-DOS 4.01		NO
MS-DOS 5.0	YES	

Don't worry if you make a mistake typing a long DR DOS command. Press the ⬆ cursor key to redisplay the command. Then use the ⬅ or ➡ cursor keys to edit the command.

You can also press the ⬆ cursor key to recall and re-use previously entered command lines.

Multiple CONFIG.SYS and AUTOEXEC.BAT support

DR DOS 6.0	YES	
MS-DOS 3.30		NO
MS-DOS 4.01		NO
MS-DOS 5.0		NO

Multiple Task Switching

DR DOS 6.0	YES	
MS-DOS 3.30		NO
MS-DOS 4.01		NO
MS-DOS 5.0	YES	

The MS-DOS Shell features a Task Swapper, while DR DOS includes TaskMAX for switching between tasks.

Password Protection

DR DOS 6.0	YES	
MS-DOS 3.30		NO
MS-DOS 4.01		NO
MS-DOS 5.0		NO

Use the PASSWORD command to easily prevent unauthorized access to files and directories.

Other new features vs MS-DOS

- DR DOS inserts commas into large numbers. For example, instead of displaying 580272 bytes, DR DOS displays 580,272 bytes.

- The TREE command will display a graphical diagram of your disk directory (Chapter 3).

- The FORMAT command works only with floppy diskettes.

- The FDISK command for formatting a hard disk is menu-driven to help prevent making a serious mistake.

Use an 80x86? DR DOS may be the answer

If you require extra RAM in your 80x86 processor, DR DOS may be your answer. DR DOS takes advantage of the unused areas of video RAM and ROM BIOS (called upper memory). MS-DOS cannot by itself use this area.

You can use the EMM386.SYS program included with DR DOS to open available RAM in upper memory. See Chapter 9 for more information.

B. DR DOS Commands

DR DOS differentiates between two types of commands: external and internal commands. We'll first list the external DR DOS commands.

DR DOS External Commands

You'll use external commands (also called transient commands) less frequently than internal commands. You must load these commands from your hard disk or diskette before you can execute them. They all have the .EXE extension.

All external commands have a help function. You can access this information by typing the command followed by the /H switch. For example, if you're not certain of the syntax for ATTRIB, type the following:

```
ATTRIB /h  Enter
```

The commands which are exclusive to DR DOS or enhanced by DR DOS appear in **bold** type. The number in parentheses refers to the chapter or section where we discuss the command.

APPEND	Sets the search path for data files (11.3).
ATTRIB	Sets or erases file attributes (3.2).
BACKUP	Makes a security copy of files, directories, hard disks and diskettes (4).
CHKDSK	Examines diskettes for possible errors (2.4).
COMMAND	Loads other command processors.
COMP	Compares two files.
CURSOR	Changes display of cursor (11.6).
DELPURGE	Frees space occupied by *pending delete* files.
DELWATCH	Saves deleted files on the disk as *pending delete* files.
DISKCOMP	Checks diskettes for same contents.

DR DOS	DISKCOPY	Copies complete diskettes (3.6).
External	**DISKMAP**	Saves a copy of the FAT (File Allocation Table) to assist with file recovery.
Commands	**DISKOPT**	Rearranges files on a disk to optimize performance.
	DOSBOOK	Starts DR DOS online documentation.
	EDITOR	Program for editing files.
	EXE2BIN	Converts EXE files into binary files.
	FASTOPEN	Increases the speed of file access.
	FC	Compares ASCII text or binary files and reports differences found.
	FDISK	Hard drive management (2.3).
	FILELINK	Data transfer between two computers (10.4).
	FIND	Displays a character string in a file (5.4).
	FORMAT	Formats a diskette (2.2).
	GRAFTABL	Displays extra and international characters with a CGA (Color Graphics) Adaptor.
	GRAPHICS	Prints a graphics screen (with Prt Sc).
	JOIN	Connects directory to a disk drive.
	KEYB	Chooses country keyboard layout (11.4).
	LABEL	Sets diskette name.
	LOCK	Temporarily locks the operating system.
	MEM	Displays information about the memory division (9.2).
	MEMMAX	Selectively disables DR DOS enhanced memory feature that may conflict with certain applications.
	MODE	Sets mode of screen, printer and interface.
	MOVE	Moves files and subdirectories to other locations.
	NLSFUNC	Loads country specific functions.

DR DOS	**PASSWORD**	Password protection for files and directories (10.2).
External		
Commands	PRINT	Prints text files.
	RECOVER	Reconstructs defective files.
	RENDIR	Renames directories.
	REPLACE	Copies selected files.
	RESTORE	Copies security copies made with BACKUP back onto the hard drive (4.2).
	SCRIPT	Postscript printer support for DR DOS 6.0.
	SETUP	Program for setting system configuration.
	SHARE	Supports file sharing.
	SID	Debugging program.
	SORT	Sorts and displays list.
	SSTOR	Starts the SuperStor program (8.6).
	SUPERPCK	Starts the Super PC-Kwik disk cache program (8.2).
	SYS	Transfers operating system files.
	TASKMAX	Permits switching between different applications (7).
	TOUCH	Changes system date and time of a file (10.5).
	TREE	Displays directory hierarchy (3.5).
	UNDELETE	Attempts to recover deleted files.
	UNFORMAT	Recovers a disk that has been "safe formatted".
	UNINSTAL	Restores old operating system.
	XCOPY	Copies file groups and directories together with its subdirectories (3.6).
	XDEL	Erases file groups and directories together with its subdirectories.
	XDIR	Displays expanded directory (3.2).

DR DOS Internal Commands

DR DOS
Internal
Commands

Internal commands are loaded into main memory when you start your computer. Since these commands reside in memory, they're available for you to use immediately.

The number in parentheses refers to the chapter(s) where we discuss the command.

ASSIGN	Connects disk drive access.
BREAK	Program interrupt with the <Break> key (11.1).
CHCP	Switches the character set table.
CHDIR/CD	Switches the current directory (3.3).
CLS	Erases the screen.
COPY	Copies files (3.6).
CTTY	Sets standard input and output devices (10.4).
DATE	Displays and changes system date (3.1).
DEL	Erases files (3.3).
DELQ	Erases files with confirmation.
DIR	Displays directory contents (3.3).
ERAQ	Erases files with confirmation.
ERASE/ERA	Erases files.
EXIT	Returns to program being executed.
HILOAD	Loads applications into memory between 640K and 1MB (9).
MKDIR/MD	Creates a directory (3.3).
MORE	Displays file page by page on screen (5.3).
PATH	Sets search path for command files (11.2).
PROMPT	Sets the system prompt (11.6).

DR DOS	RENAME	Renames or moves files (3.7).
Internal		
Commands	RMDIR/RD	Erases a directory (3.3).
	SET	Changes the system environment (11.5).
	SUBST	Assigns a directory to a drive.
	TIME	Displays and changes system time (3.1).
	TYPE	Displays a file on the screen.
	VER	Displays the current version number of DR DOS.
	VERIFY	Checks if data was written onto a diskette or hard drive correctly.
	VOL	Displays diskette/hard disk name.

C.   Glossary

3.5" diskette	A specific size of diskette. They have more storage capacity and are more rugged and portable than 5.25" diskettes.
5.25" diskette	A specific size of diskette. This type of diskette can store up to 1.2Mb of data or approximately 1,200,000 characters of text.
8086 processor	An Intel microprocessor developed in 1978. It features a full 16-bit data bus and can address 1Mb of memory.
8088 processor	An Intel microprocessor developed in 1978. It features an 8-bit external data bus (for disk drives, etc.) and an internal 16-bit data bus. It was used in the original IBM-PC computers and can address 1Mb of RAM.
80286 processor	An Intel microprocessor developed in 1984. It features a 16-bit data bus and can address 16Mb of RAM (in protected mode).
ASCII	Acronym for American Standard Code for Information Interchange. It's the standard for keyboard character codes, which applies to some extent to keyboards and printers.
AT	Acronym for Advanced Technology. The AT is essentially the "big brother" of the PC. It has a more powerful microprocessor, a higher processing speed in most cases, larger memory capacity beyond the 640K limit set by the old PC configuration and higher disk storage capacity.
AUTOEXEC.BAT	Abbreviation for AUTOEXECute BATch file. It's automatically executed when the system is started and contains commands used for tuning the system.
BACKUP	A DR DOS data protection command where the programs and data are copied, usually to a floppy diskette.
Backup copy	Duplicate of an original diskette or file.
Base memory	The first, or lower, 640K of the first megabyte of memory.
Batch file	A file containing a collection of commands. DR-DOS executes these commands in sequence when you enter the filename. It's also known as batch processing or batch job. You can create batch files by using the COPY CON command (for example, COPY CON FILE.BAT), the

EDITOR or a word processing program. Remember to use the BAT extension with any batch filename.

Baud

The unit used to measure the rate of data transmission, for example when communicating with another computer by telephone. A baud is approximately 1 bit per second. The term comes from J.M.E. Baudot, the inventor of the Baudot telegraph code. Standard baud rates include 300 baud, 1200 baud, 2400 baud, etc.

Baud rate

The baud rate gives the transfer speed of data in bits per second.

BIOS

Acronym for Basic Input Output System. BIOS is a program permanently stored in the memory of the computer and is available without an operating system diskette. For example, it performs the internal self test of the computer (counting up the memory available, and testing for connected peripherals such as disk drives). It also triggers the search for the operating system (DR-DOS) on the diskette in the drive.

Bit

The smallest unit of information in a computer. A bit stands for one piece of information, either a 0 or 1.

Boot/Reboot

The loading process which places the operating system in memory. A diskette used for booting a PC must have two "hidden" files available for telling the PC to boot, as well as the COMMAND.COM file.

Buffer

A buffer is a memory area in which data can be stored temporarily. The data can be read from or written to a diskette. Data cannot usually be read from a diskette character by character. It's read only in larger units (sectors, clusters or tracks).

Byte

A group of eight bits. While a bit can only assume two states, 0 and 1, a byte can store from 0 up to 255 conditions. Most of the time a character is stored in a byte. Therefore a byte can store up to 255 different characters. The standard ASCII character set consists of 128 characters; the additional characters generally used in PC software brings the total number of characters up to 255.

Cache

A special area of RAM to store the most frequently accessed information in RAM. You can greatly improve the speed of your system by using cache memory because it "optimizes" the cooperation among the different components of your system.

Centronics

Standard connection between the PC and a printer. The connection of other devices to the PC occurs through interfaces. These interfaces use

239

standardized connectors. There are serial interfaces, in which data is sent as individual bits, and parallel interfaces, in which a byte can be transmitted simultaneously. Both interfaces have their own standards: Centronics interfaces for parallel; RS-232 interfaces for serial. Most printers are attached through the parallel Centronics interface. It has the device designation LPT1: (Line Printer 1).

CHKDSK   Abbreviation for CHecKDiSK. An external DR DOS command, it's used to test and provide information on diskettes or the hard disks. CHKDSK also tells you of any errors on the diskette and asks you if those errors should be corrected. The remaining space on the diskette is also indicated. At the end of the display, two lines indicate the total memory available in the PC and how much memory space is still available to the user.

Clone   Another word to describe an IBM compatible computer.

Cold start   Switching the computer off and on. It's the complete shutting down and switching on again of the computer. The cold start is the last chance to have the computer start completely new. Since switching the computer off and on puts much stress on the electronic components, use the warm start whenever possible.

COMMAND.COM The COMMAND.COM is the command interpreter of the operating system. All entries by the user run through this program.

Compatible   Hardware and software which work together. A computer which is fully IBM compatible should be capable of executing all programs which exist for the IBM PC.

CONFIG.SYS   CONFIG.SYS is analyzed when the system is started and DR DOS informs the operating system of the entries in this file.

Configuration   The collection of devices which comprise the complete computer system.

Conventional memory
   See *base memory*.

Current directory To access a file or a directory, DOS uses the current directory. A directory can be made into the current directory by indicating the position relative to the current directory or giving the complete pathname. For the first case use the CD .. and CD NAME commands. In the second case, first the drive (letter and colon) and then the path through the subdirectories must be indicated, separated by the backslash.

Current drive | The standard drive or current drive is the drive to which all disk commands of the computer apply. Usually, and especially for systems with only one drive, this is drive A:. If two drives are available, the second drive can be selected with B:. This command can be reversed with A:. The hard disk drive can be selected with C:. The standard drive is displayed in the system prompt (see *Prompt*).

Cursor | A small, rectangular, blinking spot of light on the screen which marks the spot where a character is entered from the keyboard. The arrow keys (also called cursor keys) move the cursor back and forth.

DIR | DR DOS command to display the directory of the current drive. First the name of the disk appears, if present. Then the filename (with up to eight characters permitted), and, if available, an extension (maximum of three characters) appears. This is followed by the size of the file in bytes. Finally the date and time is displayed when the file was created or last modified.

Directory | A directory manages files and subdirectories and is therefore part of a storage medium. Before the hard disk drive was commonly used, all files were stored in one directory, the root directory. Because of the large capacity of the hard disk drive, a separation into various directories became necessary. They are arranged in a tree structure where the root directory can contain files and subdirectories. Every subdirectory in turn can contain files and subdirectories. Most DOS commands act only on the current directory which can be indicated with CD.

Disk drive | A disk drive is a physical unit that contains a storage media.

Diskettes | Removable data storage media. PC systems use two sizes. When purchasing new disks, make sure they are double sided and double density. Double sided means that the PC can write on both sides. Double density refers to the density of the magnetic material coating.

Empty directory | A directory containing no files or subdirectories. When the DIR command is invoked from within an empty directory, the directory display indicates entries with one or two periods and a <DIR> identifier instead of filenames. The identifier is required by DOS. Empty directories may be removed by moving up one directory level entering CD .. and entering the RD command.

Executable command
Program files with the extensions .BAT, .COM and .EXE, which you can execute directly from DR DOS.

Expanded memory   The memory area over 1Mb that can be addressed by a window under the 1MB limit. Note that this area of memory requires special drivers and works only with software written for it.

Expanded Memory Specification (EMS)
A section of RAM above the 1Mb limit set by PCs and XTs. Software and applications cannot work with EMS unless specifically written for EMS.

Extended memory   Area of memory above 1Mb which a computer using a 286, 386 or 486 processor can access.

FAT   See *File Allocation Table.*

File   A file is the smallest management object of DR DOS. Files contain programs or data and are managed in directories.

File Allocation Table (FAT)
A portion of all DOS formatted diskettes containing information on the number and location of files and available storage space.

Filename   A group of letters and numbers indicating a specific file stored in a directory. A filename consists of a name (maximum 8 characters) and the extension (maximum 3 characters). No spaces are allowed in the filename.

FORMAT   A DR DOS command to prepare a disk to store data. The FORMAT command is an external DR DOS command. Therefore, you must load it before you can use it:

FORMAT [Enter]

Formatting   Formatting prepares a diskette for working with the operating system.

Hard disk   A hermetically sealed disk drive which usually cannot be removed from the PC. Hard disks are usually built into the PC case and are usually very sensitive to shock and vibrations. Hard disks have much higher storage capacity than floppy diskettes: 30Mb hard disks are common in the PC market.

Head crash   Damage of the hard disk drive and possible loss of data. This can be caused by dropping or moving your computer while the hard drive is operating. You should always use the SHIP or PARK command to place the read/write head in an area where a head crash cannot occur.

High memory	The first 64K of the extended memory.
Keyboard	The easiest and most widely used device for data input.
Kilobyte (K)	1,024 bytes and usually abbreviated simply as K, for example, 512K.
Logical disk drive	A logical disk drive is a unit on which files and directories can be placed.
Low-level format	Also called physical format. This is the physical pattern of tracks and sectors created on a disk during formatting.
Megabyte (Mb)	1,024K and usually abbreviated simply as Mb, for example, 20Mb.
Mouse	An alternate means of cursor control. The mouse is a small box with two or three buttons on top. Moving the mouse on a table moves the cursor in the same direction on the screen. The mouse is most important for painting programs and graphic user interfaces.
Parallel interface	Centronics interface, usually leading to a printer (see *Centronics*). Parallel interfaces exchange data 8 bits at a time. LPT1: is the device designation for the first parallel interface. Additional parallel interfaces (if present) are accessed as LPT2: and LPT3:.
Parameter	Command elements of a DOS command separated from the command name by a space. The command COPY CON FILENAME uses the command name COPY and the two parameters CON and FILENAME.
Partition	A partition is an area on a hard drive. Large hard drives can be divided into multiple partitions.
Password	A file or a directory can be protected from unauthorized access with a password.
PATH	A DR DOS command to indicate the directory where DOS should search for the resident DOS commands. Without such a path, the search is limited to the current directory. PATH without a parameter displays the path which has been set.
Pathname	Indicates the location of a file or a directory on a volume. It consists of the drive specifier and subdirectories separated by a backslash. For example, a valid pathname for a file named TEXT.TXT could be:

A:\TEXT\PRIVATE\TEXT.TXT

Piping
: Sending the output of one program to be the input of a second program.

Primary DOS partition
: The main and bootable part of the hard disk. You need to create the primary DOS partition once for the hard drive.

Prompt
: The screen output that the operating system displays after every command.

RAM
: Abbreviation for Random Access Memory. This is memory in which data is temporarily stored. Unlike ROM, you can both write to and read from RAM. The contents of RAM are lost when the computer is switched off. See *ROM*.

RAM disk
: The title RAM disk or electronic drive refers to a memory area that simulates a disk drive for DR DOS. Access to an electronic drive is the same as access to a physical drive except that the electronic drive is much faster.

ROM
: Abbreviation for Read-Only Memory. ROM consists of information permanently saved on a chip which remains intact even after the computer is switched off. Your PC reads the information in ROM when you switch the computer on. Unlike RAM, you cannot write to ROM.

Root directory
: The main directory, as found on either a floppy disk or a hard disk drive. It is the highest level directory. This root directory can be accessed by entering the drive letter, the colon and a backslash. The root directory of drive A: can be displayed with the command:

```
DIR C:\ Enter
```

Sector
: A small portion of the track on a disk. It's the area the computer uses to store data at specific locations on the disk for retrieval. Normal PC sectors contain 512K of usable area.

Serial interface
: The serial interface is a unit for data transfer that sends the individual data bits one after another through one data connection. The mouse or a modem are the main uses for a serial interface.

Storage capacity	The quantity of data the computer can store and access internally. The PC generally has from about 256,000 up to 1,000,000 characters (256K to 1 Megabyte=1000 kilobytes) of memory capacity.
Subdirectory	Refers to a relative directory stored within another directory. For example, the following path refers to drive A:, the TEXT directory, the PRIVATE subdirectory contained within the TEXT directory and the GIFTS subdirectory contained within the PRIVATE subdirectory:

`A:\TEXT\PRIVATE\GIFTS` (Enter)

System prompt	See *prompt*.
Target disk	Also called the destination disk. It's the disk which is to receive data during the backup procedure.
Track	One of several concentric rings encoded on a disk during the low-level format. The tracks allow the computer to store data at specific locations on the disk. See also *Sector*.
User interface	The communication point between the user and the computer. In DR DOS, command entry occurs through the keyboard or through a mouse (ViewMAX).
Upper memory	The memory area between 640K and 1MB.
Utility	Programs which either help you program more efficiently or act as tools in disk and file management. Some utilities optimize the performance of a hard disk, others help the user recover deleted or destroyed files.
Wildcards	The placeholder characters "?" and "*" are wildcards. "?" stands for an individual character and "*" stands for the rest of a name or extension.
Warm start	Deletes the contents of memory and restarts the system without reloading the BIOS. Pressing (Ctrl)+(Alt)+(Del) restarts the computer.
Write	The process of storing data, usually onto a hard disk or floppy disk drive.
Write protect	Protects disks from accidental formatting or file deletion.

D. ASCII Table

Dec	Hex	Char	Dec	Hex	Char	Dec	Hex	Char	Dec	Hex	Char
0	00		32	20		64	40	@	96	60	`
1	01	☻	33	21	!	65	41	A	97	61	a
2	02	●	34	22	"	66	42	B	98	62	b
3	03	♥	35	23	#	67	43	C	99	63	c
4	04	♦	36	24	$	68	44	D	100	64	d
5	05	♣	37	25	%	69	45	E	101	65	e
6	06	♠	38	26	&	70	46	F	102	66	f
7	07	•	39	27	'	71	47	G	103	67	g
8	08	◘	40	28	(	72	48	H	104	68	h
9	09	o	41	29	)	73	49	I	105	69	i
10	0A	j	42	2A	*	74	4A	J	106	6A	j
11	0B	k	43	2B	+	75	4B	K	107	6B	k
12	0C	l	44	2C	,	76	4C	L	108	6C	l
13	0D	m	45	2D	-	77	4D	M	109	6D	m
14	0E	♪	46	2E	.	78	4E	N	110	6E	n
15	0F	☼	47	2F	/	79	4F	O	111	6F	o
16	10	►	48	30	0	80	50	P	112	70	p
17	11	◄	49	31	1	81	51	Q	113	71	q
18	12	↕	50	32	2	82	52	R	114	72	r
19	13	‼	51	33	3	83	53	S	115	73	s
20	14	¶	52	34	4	84	54	T	116	74	t
21	15	§	53	35	5	85	55	U	117	75	u
22	16	▬	54	36	6	86	56	V	118	76	v
23	17	↨	55	37	7	87	57	W	119	77	w
24	18	↑	56	38	8	88	58	X	120	78	x
25	19	↓	57	39	9	89	59	Y	121	79	y
26	1A	→	58	3A	:	90	5A	Z	122	7A	z
27	1B	←	59	3B	;	91	5B	[	123	7B	{
28	1C	∟	60	3C	<	92	5C	\	124	7C		
29	1D	↔	61	3D	=	93	5D	]	125	7D	}
30	1E	O	62	3E	>	94	5E	^	126	7E	~
31	1F	P	63	3F	?	95	5F	_	127	7F	Δ

Dec	Hex	Char	Dec	Hex	Char	Dec	Hex	Char	Dec	Hex	Char
128	80	Ç	160	A0	á	192	C0	└	224	E0	α
129	81	ü	161	A1	í	193	C1	┴	225	E1	β
130	82	é	162	A2	ó	194	C2	┬	226	E2	Γ
131	83	â	163	A3	ú	195	C3	├	227	E3	π
132	84	ä	164	A4	ñ	196	C4	─	228	E4	Σ
133	85	à	165	A5	Ñ	197	C5	┼	229	E5	σ
134	86	å	166	A6	ª	198	C6	╞	230	E6	µ
135	87	ç	167	A7	º	199	C7	╟	231	E7	τ
136	88	ê	168	A8	¿	200	C8	╚	232	E8	Φ
137	89	ë	169	A9	⌐	201	C9	╔	233	E9	θ
138	8A	è	170	AA	¬	202	CA	╩	234	EA	Ω
139	8B	ï	171	AB	½	203	CB	╦	235	EB	δ
140	8C	î	172	AC	¼	204	CC	╠	236	EC	∞
141	8D	ì	173	AD	¡	205	CD	═	237	ED	Ø
142	8E	Ä	174	AE	«	206	CE	╬	238	EE	∈
143	8F	Å	175	AF	»	207	CF	╧	239	EF	∩
144	90	É	176	B0	░	208	D0	╨	240	F0	≡
145	91	æ	177	B1	▒	209	D1	╤	241	F1	±
146	92	Æ	178	B2	▓	210	D2	╥	242	F2	≥
147	93	ô	179	B3	│	211	D3	╙	243	F3	≤
148	94	ö	180	B4	┤	212	D4	╘	244	F4	⌠
149	95	ò	181	B5	╡	213	D5	╒	245	F5	⌡
150	96	û	182	B6	╢	214	D6	╓	246	F6	÷
151	97	ù	183	B7	╖	215	D7	╫	247	F7	≈
152	98	ÿ	184	B8	╕	216	D8	╪	248	F8	°
153	99	Ö	185	B9	╣	217	D9	┘	249	F9	•
154	9A	Ü	186	BA	║	218	DA	┌	250	FA	·
155	9B	¢	187	BB	╗	219	DB	█	251	FB	√
156	9C	£	188	BC	╝	220	DC	▄	252	FC	ⁿ
157	9D	¥	189	BD	╜	221	DD	▌	253	FD	²
158	9E	₧	190	BE	╛	222	DE	▐	254	FE	■
159	9F	ƒ	191	BF	┐	223	DF	▀	255	FF	

Index

@ 211

A

ANSI.SYS 188, 201-204
APPEND............................. 62, 194
ASCII 141, 238, 246-247
ASCII Table..........................246-247
AT..238
ATTRIB 47-48
AUTOEXEC.BAT..... 86, 123, 214, 238

B

BACKUP...........................67-69, 238
Backup copy...............................238
Bank switching 145
Base memory..................143, 150, 238
Basic Input/Output System (BIOS) ...140
Batch file commands 211-213
Batch file variables.......................210
Batch files......................209-215, 238
Baud rate 172-173, 239
Binary system 140
BIOS....................140, 150, 239
Bits............................140, 173, 239
Block device 188
Boot record............................... 32
Boot/Reboot...............................239
BREAK....................................184
Buffer.............................185, 239
BUFFERS 185
Byte...............................140, 239

C

Cache.......................................239
Calculator 97-98
CALL 211
CD 50
Centronics.................................239
CHAIN.....................................186

CHDIR.................................... 50
CHKDSK 36-37, 67, 77, 214, 240
Clock.................................... 99
Clone....................................240
Cold start................................240
COMMAND.COM.................150, 240
Compatible hardware......................240
CON....................................200
CONFIG.SYS 78, 183-192, 200, 240
Configuration 240
Conventional memory............143, 240
COPY CON..............................209
COUNTRY..............................186
CPOS 187
CTTY 174-175
Current directory..........................240
Current drive.............................241
CURSOR 179
Cursor...................................241

D

Data storage................................ 27
DATE 44-45, 178, 214
DEL...................................51-52
DELPURGE.............................121
DELWATCH.............................121
DEVICE.................................187
Device drivers 187, 200
Dialogs..............................100-102
DIR 41, 209, 241
Directory.................................241
Disk cache...............................119
Disk compression.........................127
Disk drives...........................27, 241
DISKCOPY 59, 118
Diskette formatting.....................32-33
Diskette handling.....................29-30
Diskettes....................28-33, 238, 241
DISKMAP...............................123
DiskMAX...........................3, 117
DISKOPT...............................124

DISPLAY.SYS.............................200
DOSBOOK..................................180
DRIVER.SYS 200
DRIVPARM 188

E

ECHO.................................188, 211
EDITOR......................159-164, 209
EMM386.SYS...........................154
EMMXMA.SYS.........................156
Empty directory.............................241
EMS-see *Expanded Memory Specification*
Environment space..................192, 196
Error messages.......................219-224
Executable command.....................242
EXIT....................................188
Expanded memory......118, 145-147, 242
Extended memory 109, 118, 144, 242
Extension.......................................41
External commands 22

F

FASTOPEN...................................188
FAT (File Allocation Table).....123, 242
FCBS..189
FDISK 6, 34
File..242
File Allocation Table (FAT).....123, 242
File attribute................................ 47
File Copy... (ViewMAX)................101
File exchange...............................172
File extension................................ 42
File Info/Rename... (ViewMAX)......101
File menu (ViewMAX)................... 91
File structure 49
FILELINK 4, 172-177
Filename............................. 41, 242
FILES 189
Filter commands........................... 75
FIND 75-76, 81
Floppy disk drives 27
Floppy diskettes—see *Diskettes*
FOR 211
FORMAT..........................118, 242
Formatting disks 32-35, 242

G-H

Global..................................166
GOSUB..................................189
GOTO............................190, 211
Graphical user interface................ 85
Hard disks 27, 34-35, 242
    formatting..................34-35
    optimizing 124
    partitioning 34
HD (High Density) 31
Head crash.............................242
Help.........................22, 161, 180
Help menu (ViewMAX)................. 96
HIBUFFERS..............................190
Hidden files 57
HIDEVICE...............................190
HIDOS.SYS.................152, 190, 200
Hierarchical file structure................ 49
High Density (HD) 31
High Memory Area (HMA) 107, 145
HIINSTALL...............................190
HISTORY........17, 20-22, 183, 190-191
HMA (High Memory Area) 107, 145

I-M

IF..212
INSTALL 5-14, 191
Internal commands 22
Keyboard....................................243
LABEL......................................211
LASTDRIVE...............................191
Logical disk drive 35, 243
Low-level format..........................243
LPT1 200
MD... 49
MEM..............................148-149
Memory disk 118, 183
Memory management.......139, 141, 151
Memory Page Frame.....................146
MemoryMAX.........................3, 142
MKDIR 49
MORE 75, 80
Mouse....................................243

O-P

Operating system................................3
Options menu (ViewMAX) 93
Parallel interface....................200, 243
Parameter.......................................243
Parity bit................................172-173
Partition 34, 243
PASSWORD...........................165-167
PATH 54, 72, 166, 215, 243
PAUSE 212
Pending delete files 121
Pipe.............................. 76, 174, 244
Primary DOS partition 244
PRINTER.SYS...............................200
PRN 200
Processor 238
PROMPT 123, 198-199, 244
Protected mode...............................144

R

RAM disk........118, 183, 188, 204, 244
RAM—see *Random Access Memory*
Random Access Memory...139, 144, 244
RD 51
Read-Only Memory.........................139
Real mode......................................144
RECEIVE.......................................177
Redirect data 76-77
REM.......................................191, 212
RESTORE.............................67, 70-71
RETURN.......................................192
RMDIR... 51
ROM 139-140, 144, 244
Root directory...................32, 50, 244

S

Scrolling.. 42
Sectors 28, 244
Security.................................... 3, 168
Serial interface 172, 244
SET..................123, 192, 196-197
SETUP........17, 86, 107, 117, 183, 200
Shadow RAM 144

SHELL...192
SHIFT..213
Slave..172
SORT 75-79
Source diskette.............................. 57
Split-window mode........................ 87
SSTOR.EXE.................................128
SSTORDRV.SYS..........................128
Stop bit...............................172, 173
Storage capacity 245
Subdirectory 51, 58, 245
Super PC-Kwik Disk Cache 119
SUPERPCK...................................119
SuperStor......................................127
SWITCH 192
System prompt 245
System startup...............................150

T

Target diskette........................ 57, 245
TaskMAX...........................3, 107-114
TIME.....................44-46, 178, 214
TIMEOUT 192
TOUCH...178
Tracks 28, 245
Transient commands...................... 22
TRANSMIT...................................177
TREE.. 55
TSR..121
TYPE.. 75

U-Z

Upper memory.....................143, 245
User interface................................245
Utilities.........................159-179, 245
VDISK.SYS......118, 188, 200, 204-205
View menu (ViewMAX)................. 95
ViewMAX 3, 85-101
ViewMAX menu (ViewMAX) 97-99
Virtual disk 118, 183, 188, 204, 244
Warm start....................................245
Wildcards 60, 245
Write protect...................... 30, 245
XCOPY... 58
XDIR.. 48

?

pc catalog

Order Toll Free 1-800-451-4319

5370 52nd Street SE • Grand Rapids, MI 49512
Phone: (616) 698-0330 • Fax: (616) 698-0325

Beginners Series books remove the confusing jargon and get you up and running quickly with your PC.

PC and Compatible Computers for Beginners - For the absolute newcomer to personal computers. Describes the PC and all of its components in a non-technical way. Introduces DOS commands.
ISBN 1-55755-060-3 $18.95
Canada: 52072 $22.95

MS-DOS for Beginners - Describes the most important DOS commands clearly and understandably. Teaches skills required to use your PC more effectively.
ISBN 1-55755-061-1 $18.95
Canada: 52071 $22.95

UNIX for Beginners - Clearly describes this popular operating system, Logon procedures, file concepts and commands using simple and clear examples.
ISBN 1-55755-065-4 $18.95
Canada: 52073 $22.95

Lotus 1-2-3 for Beginners - Presents the basics with examples, clearly, without using confusing 'computer jargon'. Includes Release 2.2 information.
ISBN 1-55755-066-2 $18.95
Canada: 52069 $22.9

GW-BASIC Programming for Beginners* - A simple introduction to programming the PC using the BASIC language. Learn many of the commands writing sample programs and taking chapter quizzes.
ISBN 1-55755-062-X $18.95
Canada: 52068 $22.95

*Companion Disk available for $14.95 each ($19.95 CDN)

To order direct call Toll Free 1-800-451-4319
In US and Canada add $5.00 shipping and handling. Foreign orders add $13.00 per item.
Michigan residents add 4% sales tax.

Word for Windows Know-How

Microsoft Word for Windows is considered the premier wordprocessor among Windows users. This book is not only a guide to using Word for Windows, it also presents many important techniques for exploiting all of the powerful features in this package. Learn about working with macros; handling graphics; printer formatting and more. Includes complete details on the new Word BASIC and companion disk that contains style sheets, Word BASIC examples, macros and much more.
ISBN 1-55755-093-X. $34.95
Canada: 53924 $45.95

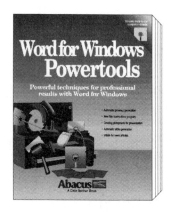

Word for Windows Powertools

contains many tools including ready-to-use style templates and printer files for beginners and advanced users who demand professional results. All of these tools can be easily integrated with your other Windows applications. You'll learn important elements of programming in WordBASIC and Word's macro language.

Word for Windows Powertools comes with companion disk containing many style sheets and more.

ISBN 1-55755-103-0. Suggested retail price $34.95.
Canada: 53924 $45.95

Productivity Series books are for users who want to become more productive with their PC.

Tips & Tricks for your PC Printer

Describes how printers work, basic printer configurations using DIP switches, using MS-DOS commands for simple printer control. Includes utilities on a 5.25" companion diskette to demonstrate popular software commands. Useful printer accessories, font editor and printing tricks and tips. 400 pp. with companion disk containing essential printer utilities.

ISBN 1-55755-075-1. $34.95

Canada: 53903 $45.95

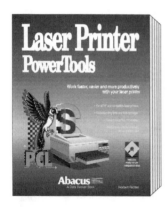

Laser Printer PowerTools

shows you how to harness all the capabilities built into your HP-compatible laser printer quickly and easily. You'll learn about both the built-in and add-on fonts, the whys and hows of printing graphics, understanding the Printer Control Language (PCL) and how to set up dozens of applications to get the most from your laser printer. The companion disk includes programs for printing ASCII files, initializing margins and fonts; printing soft fonts, using Word printer drivers, converting ASCII files to print characters. It also includes many sample files you can use to get the most out of your printer.

350 page book with companion disk.

ISBN 1-55755-095-6 $34.95

Canada: 53925 $45.95

To order direct call Toll Free 1-800-451-4319

In US and Canada add $5.00 shipping and handling. Foreign orders add $13.00 per item.
Michigan residents add 4% sales tax.

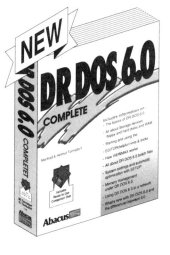

Upgrading & Maintaining your PC

Your PC represents a major investment. This book shows you how to turn your PC into a high performance computing machine. It describes what you'll see when you open the "hood" and how all of the parts work together. Whether you want to add a hard drive, increase your memory, upgrade to a higher resolution monitor, or turn your XT into a fast AT or 386 screamer, you'll see how to do it easily and economically, without having to be an electronics wizard.

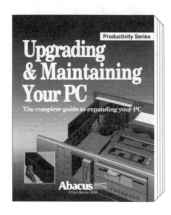

ISBN 1-55755-092-1. $24.95
Canada: 53926 $33.95

Batch files make your computer sessions easier. **Batch File Powertools** shows you how to use powerful, easy-to-learn techniques for many DOS applications. You'll boost your computing productivity with these techniques for making truly powerful batch files. **Batch File Powertools** includes dozens of new batch commands for writing time-saving, easy-to-use "power" batch files.

Batch File Powertools includes BatchBASIC on the companion disk. BatchBASIC adds dozens of new commands to DOS to help increase your computing productivity. The companion disk also contains dozens of practical examples.
ISBN 1-55755-102-2. $34.95
Canada: $45.95

PC Paintbrush Complete

PC Paintbrush has been a bestseller for several years. This book shows you how to use features of all versions of this popular painting and design software including the newest, Version IV Plus. Not only does it describe all the features of PC Paintbrush, it also includes detailed hints and examples. Contains technical information: file memory requirements, and how to use other input devices (scanners, mouse, joystick, etc.). Paintbrush utilities and more. ISBN 1-55755-097-2. $19.95
Canada: 53923 $24.95

Finding (Almost) Free Software

A unique reference guide to the most popular public domain and shareware programs available today. Contains hints and tips for applications including wordprocessing, spreadsheets, graphics, telecommunications, databases, printer utilities, font utilities, compression and archiving programs, games and much more. 240 pp.
ISBN 1-55755-090-5. $16.95
Canada: 54386 $22.95

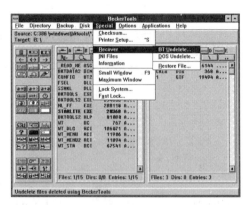

Universal Data Transfer Cable

A Universal Data Transfer null modem cable for use with the DR DOS FILELINK program is available directly from Abacus. This cable is a multiple head cable so it will allow data transfer between most IBM compatible desktop computers and laptop computers using the FILELINK data transfer software of DR DOS.

This special 4 headed cable allows data transfers using FILELINK between any two IBM compatible PCs with a 9 pin or 25 pin serial port. The Universal Data Transfer interface cable includes a 9-pin-female/25-pin-female to 9-pin-female/25-pin-female 4 headed cable.

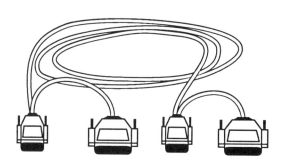

Universal Data Transfer null modem cable $24.95
Shipping and handling $ 5.00
Plus applicable sales tax (MI 4%)   ———

        Total enclosed: ———

I prefer to pay as follows:
☐ Check or money order enclosed
☐ MasterCard   ☐ Visa   ☐ American Express
Card No: _____
Card Holder name:_____
Signature: _____

Ship to: _____
Company: _____
Address:_____
City, State, Zip: _____
Daytime phone: _____

Order NOW! **To order direct call Toll Free 1-800-451-4319**
    Fax this order blank to 1-616-698-0325 or mail it to:

5370 52nd Street SE • Grand Rapids, MI 49512
Phone (616) 698-0330 • FAX (616) 698-0325

 **Digital Research** ®

Get the Best Thing that Ever Happened to DOS for a Special Price

DR DOS ™ 6.0 ORDER FORM

YES, I've read all about DR DOS 6.0 and now I want it! Please rush me one copy of the full DR DOS 6.0 product, direct from Digital Research Inc., at the special discount price of $49*, that's a **$50 savings** off the $99 Suggested Retail Price.

·I understand that DR DOS 6.0 is the most advanced, fully DOS-compatible operating system available and will help me get more out of my PC's processor, memory, and hard disk. I realize that I can return DR DOS 6.0 within 60 days of receipt for a full refund if I'm not completely satisfied. (Offer valid through June 30, 1992 - Includes Software User's Guide, and Quick Reference Guide)

DR DOS 6.0	$ 49
Shipping and handling	$ 9.95
Plus applicable sales tax in following states	$ _____
MA 5%, TX 7.75%, CA 7.75%, IL 6.25%, VT 5%	
Total enclosed:	_____

I prefer to pay as follows:

☐ Check or money order enclosed

☐ MasterCard ☐ VISA ☐ AmEx

Card No.:_____ Exp. Date:_____

Card Holder Name _____

Signature _____
(all orders must be signed)

Ship to: _____

Company Name: _____

Street:_____

City_____ State_____ Zip_____

Daytime Phone:_____ FAX _____

ORDER NOW! Complete this coupon and fax to: (408) 649-8209

Or send to: Digital Research • Box DRI • Monterey, CA 93942 • (408) 647-6675 *(orders are subject to acceptance) ***plus shipping & handling***

Digital Research is a registered trademark, and the Digital Research logo and DR DOS are trademarks of Digital Research Inc. Copyright © 1991, Digital Research Inc.